Personal Best

Personal Best

MAKERS ON THEIR POEMS THAT MATTER MOST

Edited by
Erin Belieu and Carl Phillips

Copper Canyon Press
Port Townsend, Washington

Cover art: Dario Robleto, *Untitled (Shadows Evade the Sun I)*, 2012, 21 × 19 inches
paper size. Suite of 9 archival digital and lithographic prints on Hahnemühle Pearl
paper mounted on mat board. Collection of stage lights sourced from fan-shot
concert photographs (Johnny Cash, Dizzy Gillespie, Sam Cooke, Lena Horne,
Charlie Parker, Janis Joplin, Ella Fitzgerald, The Doors, Elvis Presley), edition 17/25,
4⁵⁄₁₆ × 3¾ inches. © Dario Robleto. Photo © The Museum of Fine Arts, Houston;
Albert Sanchez.

Copper Canyon Press is in residence at Fort Worden State Park in Port Townsend,
Washington, under the auspices of Centrum. Centrum is a gathering place for
artists and creative thinkers from around the world, students of all ages and back-
grounds, and audiences seeking extraordinary cultural enrichment.

LIBRARY OF CONGRESS CATALOGING-IN-PUBLICATION DATA
Names: Belieu, Erin, 1965- editor. | Phillips, Carl, 1959- editor.
Title: Personal best : makers on their poems that matter most / edited by
    Erin Belieu and Carl Phillips.
Description: Port Townsend, Washington : Copper Canyon Press, 2023. |
    Summary: "An anthology of poems edited by Erin Belieu and Carl
    Phillips"— Provided by publisher.
Identifiers: LCCN 2023021346 (print) | LCCN 2023021347 (ebook) |
    ISBN 9781556596520 (paperback) | ISBN 9781619322844 (epub)
Subjects: LCSH: American poetry—21st century. | American
    poetry—20th century. | Poetry—Authorship. | LCGFT: Poetry. |
    Essays. | Literary criticism.
Classification: LCC PS617 .P46 2023 (print) | LCC PS617 (ebook) |
    DDC 811/.608—dc23/eng/20230719
LC record available at https://lccn.loc.gov/2023021346
LC ebook record available at https://lccn.loc.gov/2023021347

9 8 7 6 5 4 3 2 FIRST PRINTING

COPPER CANYON PRESS
Post Office Box 271
Port Townsend, Washington 98368
www.coppercanyonpress.org

To Our Students

Contents

Introduction   xiii

Samuel Ace   3
I met a man

Kaveh Akbar   6
Reading Farrokhzad in a Pandemic

Rick Barot   11
The Names

Oliver Baez Bendorf   14
Untitled [Who cut me from / growing into a buck?]

Reginald Dwayne Betts   17
from *House of Unending*

Mark Bibbins   21
At the End of the Endless Decade

Jericho Brown   24
Pause

Molly McCully Brown   27
God is Your Shoulder

Victoria Chang   31
The Clock

Jos Charles   35
from *feeld*

John Lee Clark   38
Line of Descent

Martha Collins   43
White Paper 6

CAConrad   47
9 Shard

Eduardo C. Corral   50
Acquired Immune Deficiency Syndrome

Laura Da'   54
River City

Oliver de la Paz   57
The Surgical Theater as Spirit Cabinet

Mark Doty   62
No

Rita Dove   66
Götterdämmerung

Camille T. Dungy   70
Natural History

Heid E. Erdrich   74
The Theft Outright

Martín Espada   79
Haunt Me

Tarfia Faizullah   84
Great Material

Jennifer Elise Foerster   87
The Last Kingdom

Carolyn Forché   93
The Garden Shukkei-en

Rigoberto Gonzáles   98
Anaberto FaceTimes with His Mother

Jorie Graham   101
Why

Paul Guest   107
User's Guide to Physical Debilitation

Kimiko Hahn   111
The Unbearable Heart

francine j. harris   114
katherine with the lazy eye. short. and not a good poet.

Brenda Hillman   120
At the Solstice, a Yellow Fragment

Tyehimba Jess   125
Blood of my blood (walk away)

Ilya Kaminsky   131
Marina Tsvetaeva

Donika Kelly   134
Brood

Yusef Komunyakaa   137
Crack

Dorianne Laux   142
Arizona

Dana Levin   149
Working Methods

Ada Limón   153
Adaptation

Cate Marvin   156
My First Husband Was My Last

Adrian Matejka   164
On the B Side

Airea D. Matthews   168
Sexton Texts Tituba from a Bird Conservatory

Eileen Myles   173
My Boy's Red Hat

Craig Santos Perez   176
The Pacific Written Tradition

Robert Pinsky   180
The Robots

D.A. Powell   184
chronic

Roger Reeves   190
Something About John Coltrane

Jason Reynolds   200
*April 17, 1942, Jackie Robinson Gets His First
Major League Hit and We Still Us*

Erika L. Sánchez   203
Saudade

Diane Seuss   206
Still Life with Two Dead Peacocks and a Girl

Solmaz Sharif   210
The Master's House

Cedar Sigo   214
A Handbook of Poetic Forms

Jake Skeets   217
Maar

Danez Smith   220
waiting on you to die so i can be myself

Patricia Smith   223
Sweet Daddy

Arthur Sze   229
Sleepers

Mary Szybist   232
The Lushness of It

Ocean Vuong   235
Not Even

Monica Youn   242
Greenacre

Acknowledgments   245

About the Contributors   253

About the Editors   269

Introduction

IT WILL SURPRISE FEW to hear poets have a reputation for hoarding their discontents. Call it an occupational hazard for the "unacknowledged legislators," those who devote their lives to making an undersung art that often leaves its practitioners feeling skinless and misunderstood. For example, one of the measures of success as a poet is having one's work selected for inclusion in an anthology. Yet for many poets, as soon as they learn the happy news that their poems will be included, certain irritable and irrepressible questions creep to mind: "Why have the editors chosen these particular poems? Why not this other poem I wrote recently and like better?? Is this really my best work???" Etc. We were having some version of this (admittedly grumpy) conversation when one of us—we forget who now, but it could easily have been either—wondered aloud, "What if we always got to choose our own poems to represent us in an anthology?" To which the other replied, "That right there would make a great anthology." You hold the results in your hands.*

---

*Of course, as soon as we came up with this idea for the book, we racked our brains over whether someone had ever done such an anthology, and we couldn't think of anyone. It wasn't until after we'd assembled about half the materials that one of the contributors, in their e-mail that included their poem and essay, said that they thought it was great that we'd revived the idea behind Paul Engle and Joseph Langland's 1962 anthology *Poet's Choice,* whose cover advertises that "103 of the greatest living poets choose their favorite poem from their own work and give the reason for their choice." Once again, then, there's nothing new under the sun. But while our concept is the same, we have found upon investigation that the earlier volume—unsurprisingly, given the era—is decidedly less inclusive of so many kinds of people. It reflects the poetry landscape as it was. If anything, our anthology is a testament to how that landscape has shifted and broadened and been understood both anew and differently.

Our idea has been to bring together a diverse range of poets and have them choose a single poem that best represents a personal artistic touchstone thus far in their writing life, or maybe more broadly as a human being. Some whom we invited initially said that they couldn't choose their *best* poem (many compared it to having to choose a favorite child), but we hope our subtitle makes it clear that these are the "poems that matter most" to their makers for whatever reason, and for this moment. We know it's possible some of the poets here would choose a different poem, if asked today. And yet this anthology serves as an intimate record of what these many poets believe and have believed is most essential to engaging with their work. It is in some part these makers' *artes poeticae* reflected in the space of one poem.

Once the poet had chosen a poem, we asked for a brief essay, 500 to 1,000 words, on why they chose as they did. When young people are exposed to poetry in school, one of the hindrances is that it's too often presented as impenetrable unless you have the secret key to decode it, that there's something ethereal, disembodied about it, as well as about the poet. We hope the essays here remind that there's always a singular consciousness behind a poem, a maker with unique feelings and ways of thinking about the world. We also hope the essays serve as reminders of what poetry ultimately is: a reflection of what it is, and has been, to be an individual human being on a planet of others, and to be reminded that one is not alone but part of an ongoing community of others who also love, struggle, fear, long for, hope, and come at last to an end.

By far our hardest task as editors was choosing which poets to ask. We knew we wanted to avoid the marketing cynicism of creating yet another anthology in which the editors' idea of diversity seems narrow and underinformed; rather, why couldn't—why shouldn't—the book be as honestly and incidentally diverse as our present community of both poets and poetry readers? We also kept in mind that diversity is itself diverse in its definitions, and includes many ways of understanding identity and, by extension, artistic aesthetic: color, gender, disability, various expressions of queerness, geography, class identification, among others.

With these goals in mind, we began compiling names in late 2018. From the start, we knew we wouldn't include ourselves or any of our former or current students. We each made our separate list, comparing them for overlaps. Because a few who'd said yes ended up not following through, for various reasons, our list necessarily evolved a bit. And like all anthology editors, we were stuck making some very painful choices in leaving out poets we admire deeply (even close friends) due to space considerations and our need to balance the table of contents with a beautiful multiplicity of voices. But ultimately the struggle was worth it, as we believe the result is a dynamic collection of poets whose work, brought together, gives an especially strong sense of the richness, depth, and surprise of contemporary poetry in the United States.

It was helpful for us to keep in mind our target audience. While we know poetry readers of all kinds will find much to enjoy in our anthology, we've especially hoped to connect with younger readers, those at the age when a love for poetry is often forged, but for whom poetry can seem inaccessible instead of a meaningful pleasure. We asked our contributors, accordingly, to avoid academic jargon, to instead write as if they were sitting at a comfortable table sharing their poem with the reader. Likewise, we encouraged them to send author photos that show them, candidly, as ordinary human beings who just happen to write poems.

Some of the poets in their essays speak of how they write; others discuss why they wrote a particular poem, why they chose it, who it's for or about, why they return to it, why they rarely return to it and yet . . . What becomes clear is that poetry is surprisingly utilitarian, and that its uses are countless: to delight, to rescue, to memorialize, to create space for pain, to make sense of confusion, to argue a cause, to give language to—making briefly concrete—the various abstractions, the feelings, that uniquely define any human life . . . This happened . . . I am . . .

We hope our book makes poetry more inviting, and that a diverse group of readers will find themselves included, here, along with people unlike themselves, with whom, as it turns out, they have more in common than they might have expected or assumed. Poetry always reflects the world that it comes from, that the poems get written inside of. Poetry also makes other worlds both possible and knowable at once, and ideally sparks a lifelong desire to explore the infinite varieties of human experience—in doing so, we get to know ourselves better and to understand, and respect, the differentness in others, to understand a fellowship that doesn't so much override as include our respective differences, a fellowship of sharers in human life for a relatively brief time in a world as wondrous as it's also terrifying, as rich with sorrow as it can also be with joy.

Photo by Pinestereo

Personal Best

I met a man

I met a man who was a woman who was a man who was a woman who was a man who met a woman who met her genes who tic'd the toe who was a man who x'd the x and xx'd the y I met a friend who preferred to pi than to 3 or 3.2 the infinite slide through the river of identitude a boat he did not want to sink who met a god who was a tiny space who was a shot who was a god who was a son who was a girl who was a tree I met a god who was a sign who was a mold who fermented a new species on the pier beneath the ropes of coral

I met a man who was a fume who was a man who was a ramp who was a peril who was a woman who carried the x and x'd the y the yy who xx'd the simple torch

I rest (the man who) a woman who tells the cold who preferred a wind who was a silo a chime who met a corner a fuel an aurora a hero a final sweep

(10 years without a name an ordinary life)

Since midway through 2021, I've been living with a newborn human, a being who is for the first time seeing and feeling the world we live in. What a privilege! For so long, I've encouraged my students to write as if experiencing the world as new, before language or naming, before prior experience or expectation. When my husband was pregnant, I read poems every night to the baby in his belly. I would rarely read children's poems, but instead read from a poet whom I happened to be reading at the time, or whom I was teaching that week. Right from the beginning, our baby emerged with language—grunts, squeaks, little mumbles of sound, and vocal tiny baby dreams. I certainly don't credit this phenomenon to my prebirth nighttime ritual, as it seems that many newborns regularly vocalize. But what do babies dream? Our child clearly has definite likes and dislikes, definite boundaries, and no problem expressing what they like and dislike. What they don't have is a gender. What they don't have is a category for a gender. What they do have is an intersection with the world, some grouping of chromosomes, and a gender completely of their own, yet to be known.

From the first draft, "I met a man" felt to me like an anthem. The poem begins by stating a simple fact, a fact that right off is a lie, and one that the rest of the poem tries to correct. There is a note of contradiction, or even confusion, but the poem goes on to render the feelings of recognition that happen when one encounters someone who resonates with the deepest sense of self—the self who as yet has no name and which the subject's language has thus far failed to account for. While the poem opens with a struggle to find language, it continues on to push against the vastly imperfect categories that English provides. Who is this man who does not fit into the category of "man," but who so reflects one's sense of self that the reflection is like looking into molten metal? This is explicitly the experience of a trans or nonbinary person who tries to name what the language and the culture has tried to erase. What is that recognition, that understanding before understanding? What does it mean to recognize oneself in someone else, to intuit that one's language or culture has been lacking and incomplete, thus forcing the individual to create some new and communicable morphology of the body? As the clauses of the poem circulate, they become a rebellion, an anti-categorical attempt at clarity. The poem mixes up the chromosomal evidence and the ways in which language and biology intersect. Any attempt to arrive at an answer fails, and the poem resorts to accumulation. Words follow without pause or punctuation. There is no break, no comma, but inevitable translation and transformation. Language becomes entirely parenthetical as the poem attempts to find a path to the heart.

I wonder if our baby already knows the syllables of the poems they heard before they came into the world. Are they simply sounds or music, yet unconnected to experience? Or do they already contain some meaning? The last line of "I met a man" suggests there is a timeline for the search for a name (ten years), but that too is perhaps a lie. The actual timeline exists as a lifetime of defiance in the face of erasure.

In the end, the poem elicits a claim that "ordinary life" consists not of the most-agreed-upon understanding of gender or what is so-called normal. Instead the ordinary is found in infinite manifestation, in countless genders specific to every individual on the planet. No category is wide enough. Gender can be a tree or a chime, a fuel or an aurora. Thus the poem, which begins in contradiction, ends in a recitation of possibility and confirmation.

Reading Farrokhzad in a Pandemic

The title is a lie;
I can't read Farsi.

ما هر چه را که باید از دست داده باشیم از دست داده ایم

I can make out:

"we lose,
we lose."

I type it into a translation app:
"we have lost everything we need to lose."

In between what I read and what is written:
"need," "everything."

• • •

Here, the waving flag.
Here, the other world.

Because we need mail, people die.

• • •

Because we need groceries, people die.

I write "*we* need"
knowing *we* dilutes

. . .

my responsibility,
like watercolors dipped

in a fast river.
Get behind me, English.

. . .

When I text
ما هر چه را که باید از دست داده باشیم از دست داده ایم

to my dad he writes back,
"we have lost whatever we had to lose."

Hammering
anapests.

Whatever we
had.

People die because they look like him.
My uncle jailed, his daughter killed.

. . .

This a real fact too wretched for
letters. And yet:

My uncle jailed.

. . .

His daughter killed.

Waving world,
the other flag—

there is room in the language for being
without language.

. . .

So much of *wet* is *cold*.
So much of *diamond* is *light*.

. . .

I want both my countries
to be right

to fear me.

We have lost
whatever

we had to lose.

In looking at early drafts of "Reading Farrokhzad in a Pandemic," I found myself wondering why I kept reverting to the first-person plural: "Because *we* need mail, people die." Who was my *we*?

I was slipping into the first-person plural to hide from my own responsibility, to evade really looking at my own station. "Because *I* need mail, people die. Because *I* need groceries, people die." Maybe it would have been better to write that instead. But those lines aren't the whole story, either. What I elected to do, finally, was to leave the first-person plural in, and then also acknowledge my own ugly evasion within the same poem: "I write 'we need' / knowing we dilutes // my responsibility, / like watercolors dipped // in a fast river."

Brian Eno talks about the cracking in a blues singer's voice being the sound of emotional events "too momentous for the medium assigned to record them." The tremor of recognition, of organically witnessing in real time my own mind hiding from itself—I don't have language for that. I tried as best as I could to leave that in. To let the momentousness of my shock overwhelm the lyric.

Something about that realization cracked me open. What else was I being dishonest about? The title of the poem, for starters. "Reading Farrokhzad in a Pandemic." I love Farrokhzad, but mostly I know her through biography and translation. To "read" her would imply a fluency in Farsi—my first language—which I no longer have. I inserted a new starting couplet: "The title is a lie; / I can't read Farsi."

What else was I being dishonest about? My comfort. I was stuck in my house with my spouse and cats and books for a year of quarantine, feeling sorry for myself while around me the murderous ineptitude of my two governments—American and Iranian—was actively and directly destroying the lives of millions.

What else was I being dishonest about? My rage.

When I wrote the final stanza of this poem I thought my door would be kicked down, that I was going to be carried away for even scratching those words on a notepad. Growing up in post–9/11 America as a Muslim kid, I was conditioned to suppress such feelings, to impress upon a hostile world my docility, the harmless charm of Persian rugs and pomegranate stew. Now I've written in a book: "I want both my countries / to be right // to fear me." And nothing happened. The government didn't kick down my door to take me away. It's just a line of poetry among a bunch of other lines of poetry.

What else was I being dishonest about? My art. The poem, like prayer, points me toward the next right action. But it does not supplant it. I don't pray for the unhoused and then pat myself on the back for having been so magnanimous. I pray for the unhoused, and then I go buy socks and Clif bars to disseminate. I don't know why I expected the poem to work any differently. Rosanna Warren once wrote, "I see now, purity / was just an effect of inexperience." For me this poem was an experience, a holistic maturation of the soul.

The Names

Now it's time for the lilac, blazon of spring, the prince
of plants whose name I know only when it blooms.

The blooms called forth by a bare measure of warmth,
days that are more chill than warm, though the roots must

know, and the leaves, and the spindly trunks ganged up
by the trash bins behind our houses. The blue pointillism

in morning fog. The blue that is lavender. The blue that is
purple. The smell that is the air's sugar, the sweet

weight when you put your face near, the way you would
put it near the side of someone's head. Here the ear.

Here the nape. Here the part of flesh that has no name
at all, the part that is shining because it has slipped naming.

In the crumbling photo album, the dead toddler on a bier,
dead for decades, whose name I now carry. On another

page, the old man, also decades gone, whose same name
I now carry. The name a fossil, the calcium radiance

that I bear and will eventually give up. Again it's time
for the lilacs. The quiet beautiful things at the sides of the

rec center parking lot. The purple surge by the freeway.
The sprigs I cut from the shrub leaning towards me

from the neighbor's yard, taking them at night because
I shouldn't be taking them. The blooms that are a genius

on the kitchen table, awful because I want to eat them
with my terrible eyes, with my terrible hands. The awful

lilacs, the brief lilacs, the sweet. Here is the recklessness
I have wanted. Here is the composure I have earned.

———

One of the best-known works by Albrecht Dürer is a watercolor of a hare, which he painted in 1502. The painting is astonishing for its meticulous detail, its warm realism. The painting is now in the Albertina Museum in Vienna, Austria. And though I've never been to the Albertina or seen the actual painting, I imagine that if I went there I would spend an hour or so looking at it.

One of the deep rewards of a long look at the painting would be arriving at the hare's glossy right eye, in which Dürer has microscopically painted the reflection of the window of his studio. If you're just looking at the hare, the hare is what you'll see, and that will be illumination enough. But if you knew to look into the hare's eye and saw the window there, you would find yourself in a place that includes not just the creature but also these other unfolding complexities: Dürer himself, the space where his thinking and dreaming and feeling happened, the space where his labor happened.

The window in the hare's eye is where vision and the visionary meet. And what I find so wonderful about this little moment in Dürer's painting is that it's a secret. It's there but not there. It's like a wink, a direct gesture, from the man himself—one that happens so slyly that it barely registers.

The painting that contains a secret, and the secret itself containing other secrets—this is analogous to what I wish my poems to be these days. To me, "The Names" is a bit like Dürer's painting of the hare. It's ostensibly about one thing—the lilacs of spring—but the poem also contains a strange cargo—a meditation on my name and its legacy as something that has been assigned to numerous men in my family.

Enrique—this is my given name. It's a name that, in the earnest assimilationist fervor of my late teens, I set aside for *Rick*. It was a complicated decision to have made, though my teenaged self wasn't really aware of those complexities, and I don't judge him now for the decision. *Rick* is who I am, and so is *Enrique*. An uncle who died as a toddler was also named Enrique, and so was a great-grandfather, and surely others before them.

"The Names" is about that swerve into family history even though I'd meant to write about the lush lilacs of a particular spring. The lilac, as I mention in the poem, is one of those plants that's just a namelessly green shrubby thing when it's not in bloom. But when it blooms, you suddenly know, you remember, what the plant is. That was the poem I wanted to write, but the poem had additional plans for itself, and therefore the swerve. That swerve which is the movement of transformation. That swerve which, to my mind, is poetry itself in action.

One more thing. I see now that, in my poet's mind, the image of the lilac is never far from Walt Whitman's "When Lilacs Last in the Dooryard Bloom'd." In this way, the movement in "The Names" from description to elegy had been prepared for me by Whitman long ago. And so, Whitman is there, too—one more of the poem's secrets.

Oliver Baez Bendorf

Untitled [Who cut me from / growing into a buck?]

Who cut me from
　　growing into a buck?

Who left me
　　only horns and hips?

Still, I am a good animal.

Strong,
but not too strong.

———

This brief, untitled poem occupies a liminal position in my first collection, serving as a passageway between the first and second of the book's three sections. This book drew from my autobiographical experiences transitioning gender, set in the rural landscapes that have made me.

The word *persona* comes from the ancient Latin word for "mask," as in a theatrical mask put on by a real person, becoming part of the truth. This little verse is a loose persona poem, in the voice of a young goat that recurs throughout the book. In the poem's first four lines, I pose two questions with the goat mask on. It's a farmer who intervened in their physical form.

But persona at times permits a poet expanded expression of their own. I find myself most interested in these moments where the mask slips, or is called into question, or blurs. So this poem reverberates with another layer of meaning, in which it's the book's human speaker who poses those questions, and that same speaker is also the answer.

In both cases, goat mask on or off, reassurance follows the questions: you're enough.

That part about the poem's mask slipping shows up a few times in this book. There's another poem earlier on, "Queer Facts About Vegetables," in which a tomato addresses the joy of living between categories. In that poem, I explicitly name the insistence on persona, even as the persona wobbles: "This is still the tomato / talking to the vine, / as told to me."

As an artist, at that point in my life, I was very interested in these moments of slippage. I wanted to situate the transformation of gender as something almost natural, sharing an ecology with the unruly bodies of flora and fauna all around us. And how these processes of growth, change, and bloom bump up against human desire to manage change, to categorize, to label.

In his terrific essay "Titling a Poem, Titling Anything," Alberto Ríos makes the case for why a title is so important for helping a poem circulate, including into anthologies:

> A title, after all, represents a poem, and often when the poem is not there, as in tables of contents and in conversations and so on. The title is frequently all that we know—we know many more titles than the actual pieces they name.

What does it mean to *know* something unnameable, then, or not yet nameable? This is what I needed these poems to help me do: travel beyond that for which I already had words. Find new names for things, including myself. Sort through change, loss, and making.

At the time, I was practically haunted by these lines from *Oranges Are Not the Only Fruit* by Jeanette Winterson: "Naming is a difficult and time-consuming process; it concerns essences, and it means power."

I often say that I sent my poems ahead of me in the process of transforming my gender, exploring first in words what would later in a more bodily way come to be. Writing poems helped me to find out what I wanted and what was possible. They still do that.

Ríos offers a framework for understanding what a title can do for a poem, borrowing from nautical astronomy to suggest that titles can be an instrument for locating at one moment in time. A title, he argues, offers a starting point for a reader otherwise lost at sea.

If a title helps describe a fixed point, this poem of mine remains in motion, difficult to pin down, something like the way the memory of a dream can fall apart in daylight. Even so, the poems on either side of it—and its particular role between the book's sections—do provide a way to locate the reader. I wonder how much of that will travel now that the poem goes beyond its original context. Perhaps this essay will help do the work of locating you, dear reader.

Quite obviously, I do believe in language.

The desire for poems to have titles is perhaps not so different from the impulse to set a name to anything. It's functional, of course, but also practically spiritual. Winterson again: "But on the wild nights who can call you home? Only the one who knows your name."

And so this unnamed poem of mine has gone, till now, uncalled for, unrepresented in anthology. I've read it out loud at readings from my book, and it takes all of ten seconds.

Generously, Ríos acknowledges that even a title such as "Untitled Poem #12" does everything he wants a title to do: fixes an absolute ("#12"), identifies a floating horizon line ("poem"), and filters both of those through a lens of personal idiosyncrasy ("untitled," which nevertheless is still a title).

Even now, preparing this essay, I come face to face with what by now is a familiar conundrum to me, as I hope it is for many poets: What will I call this thing? Let the question energize. People, places, and things are wily, yet still we reach for words.

from *House of Unending*

6

The crimes that unraveled me—my banner.

Only a fool confesses to owning that fact.

Honesty a disaster; the truth bound to subtract

All my prayers, leave my words stammering.

Whiskey after prison made me crave liquor,

Amber washing my glass until I'm smacked.

The murder of crows on my arm an artifact

Of freedom: what outlasts even the jailor.

Alas, there is no baptism for me tonight.

No water to drown all these memories.

The rooms in my head keep secrets that indict

Me still; my chorus of unspoken larcenies.

You carry that knowledge into your twilight,

& live without regret for your guilty pleas.

7

& live without regret for your guilty pleas—

Shit. Mornings I rise twice: once for a count

That will not come & later with the city's

Wild birds, who find freedom without counsel.

I left prison with debts no honest man could pay.

Walked out imagining I'd lapped my troubles,

But a girl once said no to my closed ears, dismayed

That I didn't pause. Remorse can't calm those evils.

I've lost myself in some kind of algebra

That turns my life into an equation that zeroes

Out, regardless of my efforts. Algophobia

Means to fear pain. I still fear who knows

All I've done. Why regret this thing I've worn?

The sinner's bouquet; house, shredded & torn.

This poem, the last two sonnets of a crown, is one of those poems I wasn't sure I'd write. You wonder, or I wonder, whether the job of a poet is to say what needs to be said, or to be loved. And yet, I know I want to be loved. Understand that the desire to be loved leaves you writing things that make you appear deserving of love. But what if you write what needs to be said?

A few years back, I was asked to write a poem for an anthology collecting pieces contemplating the idea of a feminist utopia. I was a poet, a law student, a father, husband, son—and ain't no half of what it meant to be a feminist or want a utopia that reflected such. I remembered how Etheridge Knight once said that the only people who know what it feels like to be a woman walking a street alone at night is a juvenile who's been to prison. Prison rape jokes the only rape jokes permissible by seemingly everyone. And I went to prison as a kid. And so, I wrote a poem about a world where I wouldn't have to teach my sons about the violence that men's hands might do.

I wrote the poem thinking of my mother, who'd been assaulted just weeks after I got arrested. I'd never written or talked about her experiences in public. They belonged to her, really. And we didn't speak of them for a decade after she told me. Then, on a podcast that the two of us were invited to be on, her first time on national media, she discussed it with me for the second time. We didn't prepare for the talk. And I was taken aback. I mean, I just didn't know how to respond, besides honestly. And it was rough, thinking about the violence that a man who looks like me did to someone I love. I know other women who've been raped, had spent enough time thinking of it while in prison, had read of it in books, watched it in movies—but you want to protect your mom. And poets mostly don't carry around guns. So I've been going back to the well of this moment of discovery, talking to my mom about such a painful experience—and asked her if I could write about it. What came out of that was the *New York Times Magazine* piece, "Kamala, My Mother, and Me." That piece, was me thinking of what it means to care about how the world treats Black women, more than anything else. And though I didn't know what I would say when I began writing, I knew it wasn't a poem. Still, it asked a bunch of questions I had and have no answers to, like What do I want to happen to the person who hurt my mother?

This poem, "House of Unending," is an extension of that thinking. And it was more challenging. I'm a poet of the lyric, of the first person. And there is a tension in that, in being willing to let the voice in a poem not be mine. And then try to do justice to the disaster of that speaker's life. Once, a professor sat down with me for lunch and, having read "House of Unending," said to me how brave it was for me to admit raping someone. She was a writer, a poet. And still couldn't imagine that this "I" was not me. Didn't matter that within the context of the book she'd read, it was impossible for one person to have done everything recounted in those poems. All that mattered was autobiography, and not the working through tragedy, the way I wanted to imagine viscerally what it means to have done this thing that causes folks so much pain and to do it because the first step to stopping it is to admit it happens, for the men of this world to have this conversation because we carry that weight. She imagined that I wanted empathy for myself, shit, for anyone.

Turns out I didn't write this to explain the poem, but to wonder if there is a way to engage in a poem without desperately imagining it must be a conduit for gossip. When I first heard Bruce Springsteen sing, "I got debts that no honest man could pay," I recognized brilliance. Or when Patti Smith sings, "Jesus died for somebody's sins but not mine." I wanted this poem, the breadth of it, but these last two sonnets in particular, to capture the energy and insight and mourning and suffering and remorse of those lines. And I wanted it to do things I couldn't name, because writing the longer essay, I learned all of what I have no words for; I hoped a poem might one day fill in the gap. And I still hope.

At the End of the Endless Decade

For years had anyone needed me
to spell the word commiserate

I'd have disappointed them. I envy
people who are more excited

by etymology than I am, but not
the ones who can explain how

music works—I wonder whether
the critic who wrote

that the Cocteau Twins were the voice
of god still believes it. Why not,

what else would god sound like.
Even though I know better, when I see

the word misericordia I still think
suffering, not forgiveness;

when we commiserate we are united
not in mercy but in misery,

so let's go ahead and call this abscess
of history the Great Commiseration.

The difference
between affliction and affection

is a flick, a lick—but check
again, what lurks in the letters

is "lie," and what kind of luck
is that. As the years pile up

our friends become more vocal
about their various damages:

Won't you let me monetize
your affliction, says my friend

the corporation. When I try to enter
the name of any city

it autocorrects to Forever:
I'm spending a week in Forever,

Forever was hotter than ever
this year, Forever's expensive

but oh the museums,
and all of its misery's ours.

Some poets are happy to talk about their own work—or to write about
it, which is another way of talking—while others are more reluctant.
Although I fall into the latter category, I'd like to include something
here that might be useful, so: Did you know that the word *anthology*
comes from the Greek and means "a gathering of flowers"? Not to gen-
eralize, but since poets tend to get a kick out of such information, I

doubt this will be the last time you hear this fact from one of us. You could also think of an anthology as a gathering of roots and stems and leaves and seeds. Among its pages you might find a few thorns, or a bit of dirt clinging to roots, or a bee landing on a petal, or rain.

I wrote what would become the first and last parts of "At the End of the Endless Decade" on an airplane while I was feeling unreasonably sad and tired, then promptly forgot about them. When I came across the lines in a neglected file a year or so later, I had no problem tapping back into that generative sadness and fatigue. I squeezed the Cocteau Twins reference in there partly because the poem seemed to need a bright spot, but mostly because their music changed my life. Perhaps an odd way to say thanks, but there are worse ways.

The poem was first published (from the Latin: "to make public") as part of the Academy of American Poets Poem-a-Day series. To share your work can be a disorienting experience, but it's *very* disorienting to know that your poem is landing in the inboxes of more than 350,000 (!) people and flying around the happy hellscape of social media at the same time. If I sound ungrateful, I don't mean to; it's wonderful that the Academy supports projects like Poem-a-Day, and I'm indebted to Dana Levin for asking me to submit something when she was guest-editing the series.

A year and a half later, I saw that someone had shared the last lines of the poem on Facebook. I didn't know him personally, but I knew that he lived in another country, a country that was going through extremely difficult and depressing times. I experienced those lines as if they had been written by someone else, and I hope it doesn't sound immodest of me to say that in the moment I found them . . . moving? The poet and novelist Ben Lerner has observed that lines of poetry (I'm paraphrasing here) feel more "real" to him when they are dislodged from the context of a poem and quoted in an essay or a review. And here was a scrap of my own work—glowing silently on a terrible website that plays no small role in making millions of people miserable—feeling real to me in a way it hadn't before, perhaps because those same lines felt real enough to a stranger that he was moved to share them.

Jericho Brown

Pause

From bed to dresser drawer
And all while rolling latex down
He'd whistle, and I felt
Daily at first, a chore, a long walk
Without trees. If anyone,
I should have known—
I who hate for people to comment
That I must be happy
Just because they hear me hum.
I want to ask
If they ever heard of slavery,
The work song—the best music
Is made of subtraction,
The singer seeks an exit from the scarred body
And opens his mouth
Trying to get out.
Or at least, this is how I came to understand
Willie whistling his way into me.
What was my last name? Did he remember?
Had I said? We both wanted to be rid of desire,
How it made even the shower
A rigorous experience. It driving
My coughing Corolla across Highway 90
At the darkest time of morning. It opening
His deadbolted door.
Us splayed as if for punishment

At every corner of the carpet. Then
Pause for the condom,
Elastic ache against death
Heavy in his hand,
And something our fingernails couldn't reach
Itching out a song. He was not content.
He was not bored.
If I had known the location of my own runaway
Breath, I too would have found a blues.
Poor Willie, whistling around my last name,
Wrapping his gift in safety. Poor me, thinking
If the man moves inside me
I must be empty, if I hide
Inside the man I must be cold.

⎯⎯⎯

I love this poem because it was the first time I felt myself need what I was writing as I was writing it. I had my entire life been hearing writers say that the work should be a process of discovery, that the best way to do it was to allow one word to lead to another, one line to lead to another. All of that seemed a lie when I first began. Nothing as perfect as the poems I wanted to read could have been written so instinctively.

Also, I was afraid. Writing without any idea of what I might end up saying is still scary for me. But now, it's also exhilarating. When I started this poem, though, I was very aware of and surprised by the specificity of its opening lines. And I was also surprised that I was willing to move away from them without immediately explaining how they were connected to an overall scene. The breakthrough was that I had anything at all to say after the first sentence. I was learning to leap and pivot and meander. And that felt like . . . like writing. I was finally doing the damn thing I was born to do.

If I had been any more aware of myself, if I had planned things out, the poem wouldn't have ended up queer, and it definitely wouldn't have found a way to couch that queerness in an experience that is particularly Black. I mean I wrote the Black queer poem because I was NOT trying to write it. I was just being myself and allowing the next line to say what it must, even though every line needed to tell all my business. I just dealt with the fear as I moved forward because I had gotten to the point where the poem was more important than my fear. I had also gotten to the point where I could respect my fears while also understanding that they were either unfounded or based in a very dumb need to capitulate to the beliefs of those who would have me dead.

I remember this poem when I'm writing now because the feeling I had writing it is the feeling I work toward today. I want to know as I go that I'm finding my subject. I think that writing this poem also taught me what people mean when they say the writing is the reward. I never imagined it in anthologies or even affecting anyone in any particular way. What the poem was doing for me, the satisfaction of learning as I was working on it—that was its payment. Understanding that made me feel more powerful, more bold as a person. If I could say what needed to be said here, maybe I could always say what needed to be said. If I could enjoy writing the poem without thinking of being compensated with applause, maybe I could find use for all of my work whether or not it ever got reviewed or awarded.

Molly McCully Brown

God is Your Shoulder

Is the bone in you
the place you didn't
grow a wing the lifting
your body refuses
is God belonging you
here again & again
to the red ground
and the done daylight
and the hour when
it flares back up again
is God won't leave you
alone you can't resist
your sinew or your skin
your scapula the shape
it takes it makes you up
and up ahead is God
is your own hand reaching
out to break your fall
the way you hear it

in your joints is God

is a tiny gun you can't

outrun your weight

is God the waiting

for the impact or the

thing that breaks is God

so busy with his muscling

he cannot save the house

he's made.

FRAGMENT AND WHOLE

This poem, "God is Your Shoulder," struck me as a particularly apt choice for inclusion in an anthology of writers selecting their own most representative work, because it arose, first, out of a joke about all my *other* poems. The close friend who is my first reader returned a batch of my drafts, noting every time I'd placed the body next to the divine, with asterisks beside countless times I mentioned *scapulas* or *shoulder blades,* something or someone *shouldering* their way somewhere. "Just write a poem where God *is* a shoulder" she laughed over the telephone. "Go ahead and dispense with the distance."

Go ahead and dispense with the distance. I write a great deal about the fraught relationship between my disability and my shifting faith—the difficult yoke between body and soul—and even more about coming to understand the body itself, as a place: a country we carry with us, with porous and mutable borders. And so the collapse of the space between the corporeal and the divine felt compelling: a God of and in the body. Bound to earth and bone.

. . .

The thing I love most in a poem is frequently the same thing I love about the instant when you first wake up in the morning: the sense of suspended possibility. When you're hung somewhere between asleep and dreaming, and not quite sure which version of your life you're in. When the weather of the day is still just filtered light, gathering and scattering again behind your eyelids. When contrary things are true at once: you have a meeting to get up for, and also you can fly.

I love how, in the lyric poem, wholeness exists within the fragment, even as collected fragments yield a larger whole. How a line is both a whole world and a hinge.

Perhaps this is what strikes me about the shoulder, too. Joints, or articular surfaces, are "the connections made between bones in the body which link the skeletal system into a functional whole."* In one sense, they're just fragments, hinges and ties. But each is, in and of itself, a perfect self-contained machine: bearing weights, allowing for motions, permitting growth. The shoulder's slide is almost frictionless until it isn't.

. . .

In this poem, the phrase *is God* works the way a joint does: serving as the connective tissue that makes the body of the poem run, supplanting punctuation as the mechanism for controlling pacing, and allowing for a multiplicity of meaning. God is at once *the done daylight / and the hour when / it flares back up again.* At once *your own hand* and *a tiny gun.* At once a waiting and a breaking, a refusal and a belonging. Remember how I talked about that instant in the morning when you're not fully of the waking world yet, the way it lets irreconcilable things coexist?

But even if *is God* is a smooth engine of suspended possibility, the poem is a quarrel as much as it is a prayer: invested in the frustrations

*From "Watch Out for the Warning Signs of Join Trouble." Dr. Narendra Vaidya, 9 Aug. 2019, http://www.drnarendravaidya.in/blogwatch-out-for-the-warning-signs-ofjoint-trouble/.

of being earthbound, the maddening simultaneity of beauty and pain, and the sense of being dogged by a God you might rather not believe in, only to be abandoned at the moment of impact. In other words, it's interested in what happens when motion is *not* frictionless, when—in dispensing with the distance—there is impact, wounding, rub. What do you do when you wake all the way into the world and find you haven't grown a wing?

The Clock

The Clock—died on June 24, 2009 and
it was untimely. How many times my
father has failed the *clock test*. Once I
heard a scientist with Alzheimer's on the
radio, trying to figure out why he could
no longer draw a clock. It had to do with
the *superposition of three types.* The hours
represented by 1 to 12, the minutes where
a 1 no longer represents 1 but 5, and a 2
now represents 10, then the second
hand that measures 1 to 60. I sat at the
stoplight and thought of the clock, its
perfect circle and its *superpositions,* all
the layers of complication on a plane of
thought, yet the healthy read the clock
in one single instant without a second
thought. I think about my father and his
lack of first thoughts, how every thought
is a second or third or fourth thought,
unable to locate the first most important
thought. I wonder about the man on
the radio and how far his brain has
degenerated since. Marvel at how far our

brains allow language to wander without looking back but knowing where the pier is. If you unfold an origami swan, and flatten the paper, is the paper sad because it has seen the shape of the swan or does it aspire toward flatness, a life without creases? My father is the paper. He remembers the swan but can't name it. He no longer knows the paper swan represents an animal swan. His brain is the water the animal swan once swam in, holds everything, but when thawed, all the fish disappear. Most of the words we say have something to do with fish. And when they're gone, they're gone.

⎯

I selected "The Clock" from my 2020 book *Obit* (Copper Canyon Press) because I think it aptly represents how the poems in this book felt while I was writing them—wandering and associative. If I look back at this poem, I can almost see how one line led to another. After I explain the scientist with Alzheimer's on the radio—context and setting—I end up on "a plane of thought." Something about the word *thought* passes through to the next line to "second thought," which then passes to my father and his lack of "first thoughts." As the poem wanders around, the word *pier* appears which then must have conjured images of water, and the idea of a "swan" in the water, but my swan is a paper swan (my mother used to teach me how to make origami and enjoyed the paper arts). Toward the end of the poem, I vaguely remember getting lost in all the metaphors of the swan, fish, origami, my father's dementia brain and his garbled language, but not minding the muddied feeling that I had because I was writing into the strangeness and fluidity of language, the failure of language to fully latch onto one meaning too closely or too permanently.

This poem is from a collection that includes many "obits" or small, rectangular poems shaped like traditional newspaper obituaries. The form also follows the obit in naming something that died and a date at the front of each poem (in this case, "The Clock—died on June 24, 2009 and it was untimely"). I wrote this book after my mother died after a long illness called pulmonary fibrosis. My father, who had a stroke a while back, also appears a lot in this book.

People often ask me if the "idea" of the form/shape of the obits came first/before the poems, and it sometimes surprises people when I tell them it didn't really. I was listening to an NPR piece at a stoplight, thinking about the documentary they were discussing called *Obit,* and I had this feeling that after my mother died, so many things had died. During her illness, little things were dying all the time, too. And my father obviously lost his language, but the language would occasionally come back coherent, and then disappear again. I was intrigued by the nonlinearity of loss and also the extensiveness of loss.

I went home and wrote the first poem in the book, "My Father's Frontal Lobe—died unpeacefully of a stroke on June 24, 2009 at Scripps Memorial Hospital in San Diego, California," without any intention of writing anything else or another poem like that. But then I wrote another and another and another, and I looked up two weeks later with around seventy of these pieces. During this process, I didn't ask any questions of myself or of the pieces (which in my mind, were not poems exactly), but I just went along with the writing as each obit came out one by one. The process trumped any ideas, although the end result might not appear that way.

I had handwritten these poems across a notebook, without attention to line breaks. The physical rectangular shape did not appear until the poems made their way onto the computer. When I began to transfer them onto the computer, I began to play around with the shape. In hindsight, perhaps the obituary shape was a ghost throughout the process of writing. The poet Terrance Hayes once said in an interview: "My relationship to form is that of a bird inside of a cage, moving around." And the poet Robert Creeley said something like (I'm paraphrasing): "Strong feelings require strong containers." Something about having to start writing by naming objects or abstract ideas like a frontal lobe, secrets, a clock, hands, memory, enabled my pencil to move forward, and in retrospect, perhaps allowed me to move in the grieving process, maybe not forward, but just to move. There was also something about having invisible guardrails, like the ones one might put down for a child at a bowling alley to avoid the gutter, that allowed the poems to truly be free within that space, much like Hayes's bird, wending and winding around within a cage.

In retrospect, perhaps my initial resistance to writing about my mother's death was a resistance to the elegy because I felt that everyone had already done it better than I ever could, and elegies didn't feel quite right for my own grieving process or grieving experience. My obits more aptly capture the fragmented nature of my own grief. They also seem more anti-sentimental, anti-celebratory, and perhaps rooted more in philosophy than praise, song, or lament. In this way, my obits feel culturally different to me—they feel like more of a Chinese American experience of grieving and grief.

The poet Matthew Zapruder once said to me that my obit poems "show your thinking" and I think that best encapsulates the process of writing these poems. The thinking mind is rarely linear—it branches, then branches off of the branch, and then off of that branch, then sometimes like a little bee, thinking jumps from branch to branch, flower to flower, tree to tree, and suddenly, the writer is like a drunk bee, buzzing around on a warm spring day, unsure of where she is or where she started, but feeling full; but unlike a bee, poems (at least mine) don't need to end up at the hive or where they began.

Jos Charles

from *feeld*

XXXIX.

wen the kingdum came to me / re member the

extremitie off him / or wer u busie boping gophers

& scoureing votes / wen the deposit turnd cole / wen

cavitie ment flat lik see / wen the shaype my sirfase so

neatlie crls / invagynates me / a chylde is wut ideologie

looks lik / existinglie / & i cant tell u how hapy i am

todaye / inn the guarden / mye titend mouthe a 1000

shut inn bes / the linden timly inn its glome / i culdnt

shit for wekes / a supel rede thynge & a lone

The written poem is often mistaken for the poem itself. The printed poem, the arrangement of that work on a typeset page, even more so. And while the printed or written word is one part, a layer, of many poetries' histories, it is decidedly recent: an old fine red husk of an onion dried around an ever-growing, ever-dying, ever-green heart.

The spoken word, however, is not the heart either, but yet another layer. A poem does not exist in printed matter, spoken matter, or anything so grand as all that, but, like a piece of music, which is neither its score nor any one performance of it, something else entirely,

35

something that occurs once a bit of sound or writing becomes repeatable, moving toward its own multiplicity of performances, actual or possible. It is a promise the reader encounters in performance, whether on the page, in memory, spoken by them or another, printed, or however, and just as matter-of-factly as you're "performing" this sentence by reading it.

The heart of any poem, I mean, is very simple: it is what happens when you recognize something I did or said as something you might also say or do, or I recognize something you said or did as something I might say or do. The heart of poetry is the encounter enabled by the poem; the rest grows from there.

The printed poem then is decidedly not *the* performance but an initial performance that conditions and enables subsequent ones. This, of course, limits or implies how subsequent performances are likely to be made. For instance, the end of a line of a poem might seem like a complete thought, only for the next line to surprise with the thought continuing elsewhere, toward a different conclusion than expected. It would be hard, should one sign or read such lines aloud, not to reflect this in speech or sign. The written or printed poem implies, limits, the possible performative choices a reader might make.

In this hypothetical instance, the line break acts as a limit, signaling something without "representing" it, denotatively, in words. These limits might be wide or narrow, so opaque or conflicting as to make a poem appear meaningless, or so aligned and precise as to seem only to mean exactly one thing. A poem might also set up conflicting or complicated and overlapping limits to lead someplace else—to many things at once, contradictory things, discrete and separate things, or vague, muddy, disjointed things.

The poem included here marks when I decided first to give myself over to the latter. See, I had been wanting to write about when I was a child, when I suffered a trauma a child might, and all those half-formed or -remembered, painful to remember, memories and absences that followed me since. Yet, as I tried to write it as a story— that is, as one of trauma and healing, how I'd like to think I "see things now"—it lost the feeling I felt, that existed and was still existing in me.

Yet writing those memories as a litany or list allowed something of the feeling to persist in a way writing a story didn't.

As one example from the poem, I had a memory of a dog my family had, who would sit in quiet above these gopher holes in the shared apartment complex's yard, only to slap the gophers with his paw, one by one, out and across the lawn. This was one of the first instances I recall of that trauma-feeling, a trypophobic-like feeling, about holes and passage, about passing from one world to another, and that such a hole could be violated. It seemed, as silly as it was, formative to my relation to my own body, to shame, to fragility.

When I wrote the poem, it mirrored reading, that fundamental encounter between you and me at the heart of a poem. I saw this poem become more like a hole: a container that allowed horror and playfulness to sit together, but also the past and present, just as I sat, age seven, with both horror and playfulness in me, and just as I sit now. Were I to promise resolution, or even something as simple as "meaning," it would not only have been disingenuous—I live without resolution still—the meaninglessness I felt would be abandoned. And, worst of all, the child I was would be abandoned, not only by time and world, but by myself.

And I wanted this all in the poem, too. I wanted the past, and I wanted the present—see, we live with the past in the present—that I might carry something out. The spelling throughout the poem was meant to reflect this, too, as well as the spelling throughout the collection it's from, *feeld:* at once older than me (the poem's spelling and diction resembles a Middle English of the fourteenth or fifteenth century), younger than me (with a childlike sincerity and quickness), and yet quite like me now (like a tweet or meme). Across these limitations, because of them, I felt, I was able to reach back, to the gone.

But poems are meant to be performed, not by their authors but by you; a poem is meant to be read precisely how you read it. Expression and understanding have nothing to do with it, because we live too with the inexpressible, the misunderstood. Rather, this poem, like any, is meant to be fallen into, to be passed through, and out. And in passing through, we might carry something out: it's the falling we carry.

Line of Descent

Susannah Harrison, "Songs in the
Night by a Young Woman under Heavy
Afflictions," didn't touch him, but Morrison
Heady traveled by stage from Louisville
to touch Laura Bridgman, who
demanded that Helen Keller wash her hands. Helen
later touched many of us but didn't let us
touch her back. Thankfully Laura also
touched Angeline Fuller, who
touched Clarence J. Selby, who
touched the whole world, first in Chicago
and then in Buffalo. Who shall we
choose for next in line? John Porter
Riley. We don't know who
he may have touched. We know far more
about his white classmate, but we hope
that he touched Geraldine Lawhorn, perhaps
at an Ohio Home for the Aged and Infirm
Deaf Easter Dinner. Jerrie
touched too many to number. Robert J.
Smithdas, who was an elitist bully
hiding behind poems so beautiful they opened
checkbooks. May he tremble
in peace. Richard Kinney, who
joked that the armed forces wanted him. "The Army
wanted me to join the Navy, the Navy

wanted me to join the Marines, and the Marines
wanted me to join the Army." But his hands
oozed nicotine. I instead claim Marjorie
McGuffin Wood, "Dots and Taps," who
insisted she was no saint. She fought
until she touched every one of us
in Canada, including Mae Brown. But Mae
turned out to be Our Lady
of Untimely Death. So Marjorie kept on
touching until 1988. My father Lee
was then still in denial, so it was I who
later touched him, not him me.
Leslie Paul Peterson, whose
poems still tap my shoulders in autumn. Dear too
Melanie Ipo Kuu Bond, whom
Uncle Tim Cook called Momma Nature
because she was so down to earth. But she
called herself the Black Turtle Lady
because the race is not to the swift. It is to the
slow and sure, certain of who we are.

———

I used to read only the tables of contents of poetry books because I
loved the titles. They conjured up such beautiful imaginary poems!
Most of the actual poems left me cold. A title I loved, which was, how-
ever, attached to a warm poem, was Margaret Walker's "Dear Are the
Names That Charmed Me in My Youth." It's not her best poem, but it
is a sincere and loving tribute to the heroes of her Black community.
It planted a seed in me. That idea was preserved for many, many years,
and it was the wonderful title, not the poem itself, that spoke inces-
santly to me.

Why had it taken so long for me to write a sincere and loving tribute
to my DeafBlind forebears? I needed to first bury and put to rest my
other heritage, the Deaf one. I tried but failed to be an ASL poet. It was

the wrong heritage and the wrong language. I needed to become Deaf-Blind in a deeper way. When a new language, Protactile, sneaked up on us, I knew it was my native language because I became a Protactile poet, on top of being a poet in a second language, English. Your native language does not have to be the first one you learned, or second, or even third. It is the one that clicks, and when it does it can work retroactively to supplant everything you've acquired since your birth.

"Line of Descent" is not a Protactile poem but is, fittingly, a protactile poem in English. Unlike many other communities, the DeafBlind community has historically relied on, and still relies on, correspondence to keep in touch and conduct many social functions. The Deaf-Blind poets I mention in my poem as touching one another did so in two ways—virtually, by letter or, later, by e-mail, and in person. The line of descent would be different had I traced only those who met in person or only followed the links between correspondents. For example, I had corresponded with Robert J. Smithdas and Geraldine Lawhorn but had never met them in person. The poem would have been much shorter, going from Morrison Heady to Helen Keller to Jerrie or Bob to me. Instead, the interplay between being virtually and being corporeally in touch makes the line zigzag, stop and start, produce loose ends, and, at one point, twist on itself in a knot. But readers don't need to realize this or know who all those people are. Indeed, I wrote the poem selfishly and without any desire to explain. This is one reason "Line of Descent" is my personal best.

That is, with the emphasis on "personal" rather than "best." I have a story about what that means, featuring Melanie Ipo Kuu Bond. But first, another story. She was into genealogy and decided to search for DeafBlind relatives. Like me, she had Usher syndrome, which is a recessive gene and one of the leading DeafBlind etiologies. Unlike me, she was the only DeafBlind person in her immediate biological family. So she wondered about tracking down people in her family tree.

And she found some! One was a ninth cousin some times removed, a leader in the DeafBlind community in Connecticut named Tom Peters. They already knew each other but now joyfully embraced each other as—what? For they were already kin, DeafBlind kin. Still, it was special. They laughed because Tom was descended straight down from Thomas Hooker, the first governor of Connecticut Colony, while Melanie was a Japanese Hawaiian.

One of my fondest memories is a week of festivities where Deaf-Blind friends gathered in Lafayette, Louisiana, to join that local community's biggest annual event, the April crawfish cook-off. Tom and Melanie and others were there. Some of us were members of a Deaf-Blind poetry listserv, a gentle group that got a bit tousled when a brash young poet named John Lee Clark arrived.

Knowing that we would gather in Lafayette, I decided to sponsor and judge a poetry contest. Melanie's poem "Black Turtle Lady" impressed me. On the listserv, she expressed her surprise that I'd chosen it instead of her other entries. She thought that her best poem was the one about her younger daughter. She wrote yards and yards of verse. You could say it was like her poems were intended for a family album. "Black Turtle Lady," however, happened to have other literary aspects to recommend it.

She had been on a rambling road trip with her family when they stumbled upon a mineral-gems show in Tucson, Arizona. There, she fell in love with a jeweled black turtle. She haggled and haggled, borrowed money, put in all she could spare, and still it wasn't enough. So she waited patiently like her newfound talisman until closing time, when the dealer finally agreed to sell her the turtle. The poem closes with these lines:

> The black obsidian turtle became my special icon and treasure
> We were meant for each other, not to compete but to uplift
> The turtles came long ago to teach us to endure, to measure
> We are slow and steady, for our race is not to be swift.

After I explained why I liked this poem so much, Melanie said she was reading it in a way she'd never done before. Now she declared it as her favorite, too! It was her best poem because it was the best written, I assured her. Never mind the subject matter, I said. It's all about the writing!

Looking back with years of hard-won wisdom and with dear Melanie gone to her sweet rest, I regret saying all of that. I've come to appreciate sincerity and love in poetry, not just literary merit. I only hope that, despite my youthful arrogance in the matter, her rediscovery of her poem was a gift, as her own understanding of her other poems, her personal bests, is a gift to me, now, belatedly. In Lafayette, when I announced her as the winner and presented her with the small cash prize, we embraced as only DeafBlind kin do. I still feel the warmth of that embrace and the kiss of her lips on my hands.

White Paper 6

They lived *in the colored*
section of town, as if the White
Pages map had been crayoned,
little squares, inside the lines,

as if they too had been covered
with color, something added to what
was given, i.e. ourselves who did
not know, not even our teachers,

that they were the given, that we
were the altered, that we (who still
were they, there was no difference
yet) lost our color, slowly erased

it as we moved north where a distant
sun could not get through, and on
we went, making roads and maps
of rivers and roads, assuming

we owned it if we could draw
it and color it in and give it
a name, and still we are drawing
lines and calling them borders

and coloring in and naming
people who shall not must
not cross, who live in the colored
sections of our white minds.

⟡

"White Paper 6" is, like all the poems in my six most recent books, part
of a sequence, and as such it gains resonance from its neighbors—in
this case forty-two other poems that live in a book of numbered but
untitled poems called *White Papers.* Reading the poem in context, you
would already know that the speaker grew up in Iowa, and you would
hear the first eight words as a repetition of an earlier poem in the
book. It would also be clear that the poem is only one piece of a devel-
oping exploration of race, particularly of whiteness.

But in choosing the poem for this anthology, it occurred to me that
it also may gain something by standing alone. The theme of race is pre-
sented more subtly; the fact that it's autobiographical is less explicit.
More importantly, its singleness may invite the reader to slow down a
little, to follow its development and syntax a little more closely.

In writing *White Papers,* I wanted to address in as many ways as I
could the question of what it means to be "white." I'd done research for
my previous book, *Blue Front,* which focused on a lynching my father
witnessed as a child; now, I realized, I needed to focus on myself. I
did a lot of research on the history of race and racism, exploring how
people came to be called "white," as well as the more immediate racial
and racist history of places I've lived. But the exploration also led me
to write more autobiographically than I ever had, looking back to my
childhood in a state that was 99.3 percent white at the time. My favor-
ite poems in the book combine research and personal experience, as
this one does; for me, writing these poems has been a way of reading
myself into history.

While the identity of the *they* that opens the poem is clear, the *we*
is a little shiftier. *We* are first introduced as "what was given"—an
implicit reference to the fact that white people often assume that

we're the norm. "Our teachers" picks up on the first stanza's reference to crayons, putting us in the context of schoolchildren (and incidentally dating the speaker, since printed White Pages are almost nonexistent these days). But then the poem makes an enormous shift in both time and place, taking us back to the prehistory of *Homo sapiens*—its childhood, so to speak—in Africa: *we* are now the early humans who migrated north and "lost our color" (so we could, in an evolutionary process, more easily absorb vitamin D from the sun). Then there's more movement, taking us rapidly through the colonizing history of northern humans all the way back up to the present day. "Roads and maps" return us implicitly to the map of the first stanza, and the last stanzas' "color it in" and "coloring in" to the crayons: we're back in childhood again (as "shall not must / not" also suggests), but the children are now all of us white people who have not only segregated others but also colonized the world. This expansion from the local to the global, with the local reasserting itself in the language of the last two stanzas, is one thing that pleases me about the poem.

Although I didn't plan it, the syntactic movement of the poem pleases me, too. The poem is actually one long sentence. It starts as a simple subject-predicate clause: the first eight words could be a complete sentence. But then it starts adding subordinate clauses and modifying phrases, using repeated introductory phrases to identify its major developments: two *as if*s to develop the *colored* of the first line, three *that*s to explain what we "did not know"—and then a series of verbs that follow the *we* of the last *that* clause: *lost, erased,* and then the movement verbs, with a couple of backstitches to pick up the *we:* "and on / we went," "and still we are." *They* have all but disappeared by now (as is appropriate to the subject), but they come back in the last stanza, introduced (as *we* were earlier) by two *who* clauses.

What I've just done is something I didn't do as I was writing the poem: I've tried to diagram the sentence in words, mimicking the kind of diagramming teachers made us do when I was a kid. In this case, the diagram would probably go off the page. Which, it occurs to me, is also appropriate for the poem.

Writing poems that consist of a single sentence is something I've been doing for a while, and also offering as an exercise to students and workshop participants: it's a great way to keep you going beyond your initial impulse for a poem.

But more important to me is the exercise I might have given myself in "White Paper 6": start small and personal and go large and historical without losing track of the small. That's a lesson I learned long after I was a kid studying the map of nearly square blocks in Des Moines, Iowa, and it's one I keep learning. It's a lesson in writing, and it's a lesson in living, too.

9 Shard

our
little
places
within
are not
dungeons
remember
remember
astronomers point
satellites into space
the military points
them down at us
the inverse relationship
between love we offer
and what we give
this on and
off button
is another
opportunity
to believe
there are
only two
choices
this too
must end

A Note on the (Soma)tic Poetry Ritual for the Poem "9 Shard"

for Anne Boyer

For decades, poets have told me they write their best work when they are depressed or from the pain when a lover leaves, something that steers them into melancholy. When I teach creative writing, this often comes up, and I tell the poets in my class that I understand, but I also believe that the effect of melancholy or depression is not what we think it is.

We live our lives with our lists of daily routines, such as washing our bodies and obeying traffic signals on our way to work. There is so much to remember to get through the day. When tragedy disrupts our routines, suddenly all of our attention is centered on that loss. It is in the focus of loss where many believe they can write better: *focus,* the keyword.

It is crucial to learn that the focus that depression offers helps us write, not the depression itself. After we finally understand this, we see how we can orchestrate any focus we want, to write whenever and however we want! (Soma)tic poetry rituals have given me eyes to see the creative viability for the poems in everything around us!

Depression never again has to be a catalyst for creativity! What a relief! If I had to be depressed to write poems, I would have stopped it many years ago. After my boyfriend Earth was raped and murdered, I created a ritual to overcome my depression, getting out of the melancholy instead of romanticizing its violence on our emotional and spiritual bodies.

Poetry can improve our lives' quality if we forgo the fable of sadness and alcoholism as being the best tools for a poet. I chose one of my newest poems for this anthology because I hope my latest always to be my best. Having written poems is not as important to me as continuing to write them, because it shows me I am still living in a state of awareness. This poem encapsulates many years of understanding how to trust my audience, offering correspondences rather than connecting things for them. To me, by not entirely connecting, I am inviting the reader to write with me. The space around the poem is for the reader's imagination to flourish. Collaborating with the creativity of the reader is something I always need to trust.

The poem here is from a series I call "Shards." They result from a (Soma)tic poetry ritual currently titled "Ignition Chronicles," which has a couple of ingredients I would like to explain. During the pandemic, I am in Seattle, Washington, which is part of a rainforest. It has more rain than I have ever experienced, with an average of thirty-six inches a year. I knew that a new relationship with water would be beneficial for me for many reasons, chief among them being to expand my emotional capacity to cope with so much cloud cover. Each morning, I take my bowl of millet or rice with nuts and berries to Kinnear Park to eat beneath a pine tree. The rain filtering through the branches places a taste of pine in my bowl. A Steller's jay flies to join my ritual each morning, landing nearby to scream for a nut. It is the only voice they have, so I imagine they might mean, "Good morning," but it very much sounds like a scream to me. When I mimic their sound, they seem to approve, shaking their magnificent crest. And then I write.

Then I watch the sunrise over Elliot Bay and gather pine needles for tea later in the afternoon. Hearing the Steller's jay and crows of Seattle awaken each day reassures me that we all know to greet the power of what morning brings. Later, I watch the sunrise again in another part of the world on outdoor public webcams. I have watched the sunrise in Mecca, Tokyo, Istanbul, and other places each day, trying a different outdoor webcam, meditating on these shards of light traveling nine minutes through outer space after leaving the sun to reach us here on planet Earth. Yes, illumination and warmth arrive, but so does the help it brings to our bodies for producing critical vitamins for bone health, among other things. I drink the pine needle tea while writing with worldwide sunrise each afternoon.

Eduardo C. Corral

Acquired Immune Deficiency Syndrome

I approach a harp
    abandoned
in a harvested field.
    A deer leaps
out of the brush
    and follows me

in the rain, a scarlet
    snake wound
in its dark antlers.
    My fingers
curled around a shard
    of glass—

it's like holding the hand
    of a child.
I'll cut the harp strings
    for my mandolin,
use the frame as a window
    in a chapel
yet to be built. I'll scrape

    off its blue
lacquer, melt the flakes
    down with

a candle and ladle
 and paint
the inner curve
 of my soup bowl.

The deer passes me.
 I lower my head,
stick out my tongue
 to taste
the honey smeared
 on its hind leg.

In the field's center
 I crouch near
a boulder engraved
 with a number
and stare at a gazelle's
 blue ghost,
the rain falling through it.

I REMEMBER DAVID LAWRENCE KIRBY

I came of age in the 1980s, during the AIDS epidemic in this country. As my brown body began to shimmer with desire, I watched the bodies of gay men—in magazines, on the nightly news, in movies—wither then disappear.

. . .

Bullies in elementary school delighted, like demented Adams, in naming me: *fag, homo.* I knew I wasn't those words—the words that truly described me were softer, more powerful. This was the first time I intuited words cast more than one shadow. I knew I was gay, but I thought I could keep the fact to myself—un secreto. (It was never a secret; it was visible to others.) I was terribly lonely inside the secret—it was like marching up and down in a very narrow hallway. I couldn't reach out to others. I couldn't let in my parents, my teachers. So I kept scouring the *TV Guide* for shows featuring gay men, which during the Reagan years meant illness, death. Men struck down by an early frost. Men who refused to stop loving each other. Men with normal hearts and purple skin.

• • •

In seventh grade, I couldn't sleep. In the dark, I tackled the questions my mind reeled out. If I got AIDS, how would my parents react? What word would my father utter first? Would they kick me out of the house? If so, where would I live? In a cotton field? In the desert? How quickly does the body rot in a coffin? These questions, these nightly interrogations, are one of the reasons I'm a poet. The fear of a virus spurred my imagination: I spent countless hours inventing scenarios, conjuring up vivid imagery.

• • •

I've never forgotten a series of photographs of a gaunt gay man surrounded by his family. In one photograph, his father gently cradles his head, at the moment of death.

• • •

I spent over nine years working on my first book of poems. I desperately wanted to include poems about fearing desire, equating queerness with death, overeating because skinniness was a symptom of infection, and checking the skin above my ankles for purple patches after each shower. I wanted to include a poem about my first kiss. How I closed my eyes, like the women on television. How his lips were chapped, fleshy. But each draft felt inert. After five or so years, I realized why the poems weren't working: I was forcing language into specific memories, into narrow containers. Inside these containers, language didn't have any room to veer into the unexpected.

...

If memory is a constriction, how would I be able write about growing up during the AIDS epidemic? But asking that question brought me back to the nights where scenario after scenario rattled in my skull. My body and my mind were well acquainted with these narratives— there was no surprise in those memories for me. Not only were the memories familiar, but my interrogations were also familiar. To quote Robert Hayden, I had to find another angle of ascent.

...

The way skyward was language itself. Specifically, the term *Acquired Immune Deficiency Syndrome.* I forced myself to dwell with the words, to hear the music, to find interesting possibilities inside the term. One day, an image popped into my head: words vibrating like strings. A few weeks later, the first lines of a poem sprang forth: "I approach a harp / abandoned / in a harvested field."

Laura Da'

River City

Grasping for the home sense
of the river-city, I become
increasingly enthralled
with the heavenly city

ticking inside the clock's
lavish precincts. Hours I did not
count on becoming
the river home I long for.

Flood of settlement
subsuming the divine cities—
our rivers exiled by their rivers,
christened bucolic, baptized

for dead fathers, but not ours.
Trinity gates for each
cardinal direction draft
the divine city's parameters.

City contingent on river;
beneath the dim crust of exile
foundation stones laid
with sapphires glisten

alongside rivers buried under soybean
and wheat. No word for burial
on the river's faceted tongue
in the city where I stay.

I am following a river to its lake on foot; flooding has dissolved the
riparian margin and my shoes are darkening at the tips. There is no
language like English for telling on itself.

Since time out of mind, the lake I am walking to was called Hyas
Chuk, "Large Water," in Chinook Jargon and Xacuabs in Lushootseed.
Settlers called it Duwamish for the people whose villages on its shores
they were displacing, and then, a generation or two later, Geneva, in a
wistful nostalgia of European erasure.

On July 4, 1854, a group of men decided to call the water Lake Wash-
ington. At the north end of the water, the river gently joins in what is
now the city of Kenmore, directly atop the village of Ti'awh-ah-dees.
Villages that sustained generations on a geologic time frame lie under
the achingly brief tenures of the settler cities.

The mouth of the river is obscured by housing developments and
a golf course. Road construction blocks the trail in ribbons of garish
orange. The history of timber is still apparent in commercial endeav-
ors representing every stage of the building process and in hulking
hangars of lumber behind each shop front. Ripples of the old growth
that would have embraced the lake and followed the riverbed tease
the fogged periphery—cedars of such magnificent proportions they
seem impossible now.

Waterbirds on the river are splendid in their variety. Mallards with
their stripes of sky and moss, rigid loons, and tender buffleheads who
zip down the water currents past the great blue herons hunkered
down on the rocky outcroppings. White snowberries are plentiful in
the marshes, their color and shape like a salmon's eyes said to foretell a
strong run of chinooks in the following year.

Rippling hills and farms are gentled by the misting rain. Upland a girl kicks her pony around barrels in an arena, faster each turn and yelling out: "Time? Run time? What was my time?" The word *bucolic* lights gently into my mind and perches there. It erases the triptych of colonial theft, violence, and extraction and replaces it with a paradise of green. Each word is a tender little war that winds from my tongue through my teeth.

There is a power in naming that moves in all directions. What can a river or lake say to its people when they speak to it in a stranger's language? In Shawnee, we name our villages by our rivers. Rivers still hold their names in our language—the Scioto, the Muskingum—but our villages are covered, and our people were removed from those watersheds two hundred years ago.

All the cities on the river where I live hover over Indigenous villages. No word in English describes this haunting. This inherent challenge of living in a river city is inside my poem which holds irreconcilable worldviews and irresistible territories of longing—I want the river city of my ancestors, the river I walk today, the river I could hear in my sleep as a child, I want the twelve-gated city with its clear water, too. Currents tick with the intrusion of "the clock's / lavish precincts." To leave the river city unnamed honors its complexity and allows the possibilities that all the cities—the Shawnee city, the heavenly city, the city of the mind—can live present and whole in some space in time opening on a current to a nameless body of water.

Oliver de la Paz

The Surgical Theater as Spirit Cabinet

I am without wings and obsessed with each patient's
      dark physics—the way their eyes are the copper bells
signaling the end of intermission.

It is here I come to peel away all guarantees.
      Gurneys line the hallway, some of them empty, some
with old men or children hooked to machines whose hum
      is something I can sleep against.

If this is what I'll become, then let me turn
      into a puff of smoke. Let me hide
in the warm lining of a pocket.

Somewhere behind me, men talk through
      their masks and as they speak I feel the space
between the air and my body. It is too bright,
      and the world becomes unknowable.

There is a chasm of indifferences as I am pushed
      to the double door. It's all so rehearsed.

Before my turn, I think about what I love
      the most and remember the audience, the man
whose wallet is found in his neighbor's bustier
      or the woman's watch now on the wrist of the magician.

I know. That's not love, but a sleight of hand.
        Presto, our lives bound from out of a top hat.

Now you see me and soon I'll be sawed in two.
        My brain sets its wavelengths on the flourish
of the sorcerer's cape.

                The voice's redirection
and the sotto voce of the operating room's radio.
        There is nothing up their sleeves and

I am beginning to understand
        my body as the little curtain closes.

The magician's assistant disappears—slips
        through the trap door soundlessly—my own
thin voice the hollow slap of a hand on a cabinet.

ON "THE SURGICAL THEATER AS SPIRIT CABINET," OR PHYSICS, GHOSTS, MAGIC TRICKS, AND HEALING

After my cancer diagnosis, I had written poems about metaphor that are eventually woven into my third book of poetry, *Requiem for the Orchard*. I was quite direct about the transformations I had been experiencing. My poem "The Surgical Theater as Spirit Cabinet" arose while I was contemplating transformation, possibility, and my own mortality.

• • •

There were dozens of appointments with radiologists, I remember. Lead aprons. Paper cups that look like small closing flowers with a single irradiated pill. The anesthetized smell of hand washing over and over.

. . .

In science classes I learned about matter and how it can be neither created nor destroyed. The Law of Conservation of Mass. Anything that takes up space. Anything that exists. It doesn't just disappear. It becomes something new. I felt my body changing daily. Wondered where I was going. Wondered where had the rest of me gone?

. . .

Sometimes, when I'd look in the mirror, the tumor—roughly the size of a golf ball—would show, slightly above my collar. Nested slightly above the rim of the fabric, it was a hardened mound. My mother discovered it while sitting across from me at Casa Jaramillo. In the dim candlelight of the restaurant, her medically trained gaze looked me over and saw something changed. She reached across the table and touched my neck. She looked again at me as my mother and told me to immediately go to the doctor. In the brief light I saw her eyes shift from one color to another.

. . .

I was writing about ghosts. All sorts of ghosts—those from my past. Those on television. Those spirits who had a habit of sitting on your chest, breathing all the air in the room. Stress ghosts. Grief ghosts. Regrets. Those familial burdens. Those burdens of habit. Somehow the psychological weights of things transformed into manifestations seen out of the corner of one's eye. The conservation of something weighty into something in the periphery. Within earshot yet just out of reach.

. . .

My endocrinologist had a habit of talking to me about my work life while jabbing me with needles. The biopsy of my tumor occurred while he spoke to me about poetry. A normally gruff man of sixty, he'd soften a bit when asking for reading recommendations. He was also, strangely, good at card tricks. I imagine someone who often worked with his hands had to train his dexterity by shuffling and reshuffling the deck. Here is an ace of diamonds. There it goes. Here it comes again. I bet you didn't see that coming.

· · ·

Idly I'd channel surf as I felt my body change. I'd get sudden chills. My muscles would tighten. Meredith and I watched all sorts of shows about the supernatural and paranormal. For a time, we were deeply interested in people who ghost hunted. We'd see the ubiquitous green images of night-vision cameras capture something moving slightly off to the side. A door shutting. A window sash suddenly slamming down.

· · ·

There was plenty we didn't see coming. We didn't see how sore muscles get after a thyroid and part of a salivary gland get removed. We didn't expect that I'd need help getting dressed. That I'd constantly be cold. We didn't expect falling asleep in front of the television every day. Each new symptom. Each new need.

· · ·

The two shows Meredith and I would hover over were *Criss Angel Mindfreak* and *Ghost Hunters*. We grumbled about how terrible and how "fake" they were. The formula was the same. Would the hosts succeed in their endeavors? Would matter be created out of thin air? Would the presence of a ghost be proved or disproved? And somehow these moments of seeming transformation, fake as they seemed, were comforting. That there was always the possibility of the miracle.

· · ·

In the hallway before my ablative surgical procedure, I heard the chime of bells signaling a birth.

...

My endocrinologist held up an eight of spades as he talked me through the procedure. Telling me it's easy. He tells me to watch as he slides the eight into the deck. He shuffles the deck. Holds the deck out to me to inspect. Slaps the deck and asks me to draw a card.

...

In the poem the speaker is out of their body. In the poem it is not clear what is real. What is felt. What is seen. When the magician puts his assistant inside the spirit cabinet and turns the box around and around in front of the audience so that they can see there is no deception, we all understand that we are being deceived. And really, that is the play. We know that matter cannot be created or destroyed. When the patient moves from the hall to the operating room, the expectation is that there will be a persistence in the person.

...

The curtain to the recovery room parts with a flourish. It's my endocrinologist accompanied by a team of other doctors and my family. I'm surprised by the audience gathered at the foot of my bed. I'm given a small paper cup and told to swallow the pill. I'm told that I look good. That everything went well.

...

Spin the cabinet in front of the audience a few times. Make sure to hold the cabinet still, just a beat, to allow the assistant to crawl back into the empty space. Turn it again. Make noise. Give your cape a flourish. Give the cabinet a tap. Keep their eyes on you.

No

The children have brought their wood turtle
into the dining hall
because they want us to feel

the power they have
when they hold a house
in their own hands, want us to feel

alien lacquer and the little thrill
that he might, like God, show his face.
He's the color of ruined wallpaper,

of cognac, and he's closed,
pulled in as though he'll never come out;
nothing shows but the plummy leather

of the leg, his claws resembling clusters
of diminutive raspberries.
They know he makes night

anytime he wants, so perhaps
he feels at the center of everything,
as they do. His age,

greater than that of anyone
around the table, is a room
from which they are excluded,

though they don't mind,
since they can carry this perfect
building anywhere. They love

that he might poke out
his old, old face, but doesn't.
I think the children smell unopened,

like unlit candles, as they heft him
around the table, praise his secrecy,
holding to each adult face

his prayer,
the single word of the shell,
which is no.

———

"Mystery, secrecy, camouflage, silence," writes Jane Hirshfield in her book *Ten Windows: How Great Poems Transform the World*, "stillness, shadow, distance, opacity, withdrawal, namelessness, erasure, encryption, enigma, darkness, absence—these are the kaleidoscope names of the hidden." Perhaps because I grew up in a family where the truth about anything important was never spoken, and certainly because I spent years knowing the character of my desires, but feeling almost entirely unable to speak them, the quest for truth telling has been crucial to me as a poet. My first experience with therapy, in my twenties, was a bracing engagement in naming what I knew-without-saying about myself and my family. Bringing unacknowledged, occluded knowledge to light and to language became both an aesthetic principle and something of a road map in the direction of adult life.

I still believe it's necessary to claim what clarity we can, but I won't deny that there is something deeply alluring in Jane's litany of forms of the hidden. Life would be incomplete without those terms. If they read as cold or unwelcoming, they may also seem charged with the possibility of revelation, something larger and more daring than daily life. After all, language can only name so much, and a word often seems merely a gesture in the direction of what can't quite be said. The clarity I'd sought felt lifesaving, but one of the most memorable moments in therapy for me was a mutual arrival at some aspect of human experience we couldn't explain or analyze. Then my therapist and I became like two sitting together to contemplate a fire, or a sunset—something we could only describe together, and wonder.

This dialogue between insight and mystery informs, perhaps, the uncharacteristic poem of mine I'm considering here. "No" was written in Vermont, in 1989 or '90. I was teaching at Goddard College, a progressive school founded in the 1930s to embody the educational principles of John Dewey; sixty years later, the place was small, scrappy, and happily idiosyncratic. Writing was a strong point, and mostly done in class, because the students liked putting pen to paper in a group, where new work could be shared and admired. The writing exercises I cooked up were often things I wanted to do myself, though if I wrote along with them I usually didn't keep more than a line or two. But I'd been reading Stevens, and brought in "Thirteen Ways of Looking at a Blackbird" on a warm fall day. We sat at a long table out on the porch of a handsome old building called The Manor, a fine place to listen to Stevens. After we'd talked our way through the poem, I asked the students to choose an object of interest to them, and to write a poem in numbered sections that proposed different ways of seeing the thing they had in mind.

Goddard was just then immersed in one of its better experiments, a project to bring single mothers to campus with their children, providing housing, childcare, and scholarships to help them complete a college degree. Suddenly there were children everywhere. Either on the very day I wrote the first draft of my poem or some days before, I'd been sitting at a table in the Dining Hall at lunchtime, when a fierce and muddy little band of five- or six-year-olds came roaring into the room, tearing up to our table, the boldest of them holding up to our faces in two clenched hands the bulk of a turtle. Fairly good-sized, broader than the circumference of the boy's face, the creature had wisely withdrawn any part of itself that could be withdrawn inside the hard, reflective shell.

The metaphoric resonance of some moments arises naturally, and swiftly; this seemed a paradoxical story about power, for one thing: the children can hold, move, cajole or threaten the turtle, but they can't make him reveal himself. The more ardently they try to get him to show his face, the less he is willing to do so. Is there some hint here of the hidden, quieter life, the one whose emergence—in yourself or others—you must simply await?

The poem I wrote in class was mostly complete in its initial version, though I got rid of the structure of numbered sections in which I'd composed it, and shaped the lines into tercets, a form I love for its combination of regularity and instability. (Three lines always seem a little incomplete, so we reach for something—perhaps a rhyme in the next stanza in terza rima, or maybe just the handhold or anchor of the next stanza down. Tercets keep things moving.)

And I was done. I liked reading the poem aloud and found myself coming back to it, because in some way I liked its difference from other poems of mine, a difference I couldn't quite figure out. But here's a theory: in many of my poems a kind of proposition is arrived at, a way of looking at experience or coming to terms with reality, and that isn't what's happening here. The shell is closed, unyielding, and it promises nothing, it only says no. I am aware that I had not said that word nearly enough at that point in my life, but a purely psychological explanation would seem to rob the poem of what power it may possess. The space of the unknowable remains dark, unentered, and the world is always a larger, wilder place because of it. My impulse to resolve, to propose an answer to a question, is thwarted by this shell, which won't open even for me, who authored it. I still feel refreshed by the poem, by the way it seems to stand beside a door that won't open. You can carry the little portable house of a poem anywhere, but perhaps we should be glad that it won't always show us its face.

Götterdämmerung

A straw reed climbs the car antenna.

Beyond the tinted glass, golden waves
of grain. *Golly!* I can't help
exclaiming, and he smirks—
my born-again naturalist son
with his souped-up laptop,
dear prodigy who insists
on driving the two hours
to the jet he insists I take.
(No turboprops for this

old lady.) On good days
I feel a little meaty; on bad,
a few degrees from rancid.
(Damn knee: I used it this morning
to retrieve a spilled colander;
now every cell's blowing whistles.)

At least it's still a body.
He'd never believe it, son of mine,
but I remember what it's like
to walk the world
with no help from strangers,
not even a personal trainer
to make you feel the burn.

(Most of the time, it's flutter-heart
and Her Royal Celestial Mustache.
Most of the time I'm broth
instead of honey in the bag.)

So I wear cosmetics maliciously
now. And I like my bracelets,
even though they sound ridiculous,
clinking as I skulk through the mall,
store to store like some ancient
iron-clawed griffin—but I've never

stopped wanting to cross
the equator, or touch an elk's
horns, or sing *Tosca* or screw
James Dean in a field of wheat.
To hell with wisdom. They're all wrong:
I'll never be through with my life.

"I'LL NEVER BE THROUGH WITH MY LIFE": RESURRECTING MY POEM "GÖTTERDÄMMERUNG"

Gods always behave like the people who make them.
Zora Neale Hurston

There are some poems you hold close like a love-worn stuffed
bunny—you know they're past their prime, but you can't bear to put
them down. I'll not pick one of those for this essay. Nor will I consider
the favorites that for reason of length or serial nature wouldn't make
this anthology's cut; this includes all of the poems in *Sonata Mulat-
tica,* a book some describe as a novel in verse but I think of as more
of an opera without music. Although I look at many of those pieces
with wonderment (however did I manage that?), I can understand why

they'd be difficult to anthologize without lengthy annotation. Even the stand-alone "Ludwig van Beethoven's Return to Vienna" requires a historical footnote; besides, who expects an African American woman to assume the persona of that grand German maestro?

Which brings me to the piece I've chosen. It's another persona poem; this time, though, the speaker is an elderly female, wrinkled and ornery, the kind you see shambling around retirement communities, wearing overly bright capris and lipstick that bleeds into the furrows around her mouth. Because she doesn't mention her race, she's probably white. Buoyed by the privileges of the mainstream, she rails against the startling invisibility bestowed upon the aging; even her grown son treats her like a slightly cumbersome object. I love the spunk of this old lady, her persistence and energy, her refusal to conform to the preconceptions of others, even her rage—and she is mighty angry; she will not play nice.

When "Götterdämmerung" appeared in *On the Bus with Rosa Parks*, I was just about to turn forty-seven—in hindsight, ergo, still relatively young. (My wrinkled heroine might call it *ridiculously* young.) Because I had been raised to be polite and "take the high road"—the kind of behavior that generates ulcers and psychiatrist bills—I was a little abashed by my own poem at first, although I also secretly admired its bodacious protagonist and yearned to be more like her: rude when rudeness was called for, ferocious and determined to live and love as one pleased, damn the consequences. As I've grown older, however, I recognize more and more qualities from that tenacious firebrand in myself; good days or bad will find me doggedly paddling upstream as the sleek young'uns stroke blithely past.

To acknowledge the pummeling that aging inflicts upon the mortal coil is never a popular topic in any art form, particularly when the worldview arbiters are overwhelmingly men and the subjects under scrutiny are women. Male discomfiture intensifies when the female object of derision refuses to "go gentle into that good night" and, unlike Dylan Thomas, declines to "rage against the dying of the light." The old lady in my poem insists upon her Cecil DeMille close-up, fully cognizant of where life has plopped her; she relishes gaudy jewelry and wears excessive makeup without shame. As if that weren't enough disdain poured onto the musty powdered wigs of this self-styled canonical court, she looks down on her son's display of the latest flash and trash, recognizing that his smug solicitude is simply the best he can do. Hers is the benign indulgence of a deity—that mixture of love and pity usually associated with nursing homes, packaged and sold as "compassionate care."

Perhaps the poem has eluded the anthologist's eye because it may not be seen as "representational"—that is, lacking a perspective that can resonate with humankind at large. (As if "The Love Song of J. Alfred Prufrock" could be considered gender- and diversity-friendly!) Another editor might cite its "shuttered point-of-view" as grounds for dismissal, but to claim that the speaker can't be trusted is to follow an equally disingenuous line of reasoning in which the literary trope so celebrated in Robert Browning's "My Last Duchess," that of the Unreliable Narrator, becomes code-speak here for: How could a nice Black girl like Rita Dove possibly crawl into the psyche of a cranky white bitch, then dare to equate her with Gods in Valhalla?

Ah—but inside, I am not as nice as I appear to be. I've never appreciated the struggle to be polite or understanding in the face of insensitive remarks or mean-spirited actions, and, lately, I've stopped trying. Now that my age has also consigned me to the fog-obscured Vale of the Elders, there's no need to show patience toward such careless stupidity. Like the speaker in "Describe Yourself in Three Words or Less," which appeared five years later in my collection *American Smooth,* I am "itchy and pug-willed, / gnarled and wrong-headed, / never amorous but possessing / a wild, thatched soul."

Truth be told, I never expected to see "Götterdämmerung" anthologized, for all the reasons and rants above. But if we can muster empathy for Prufrock's rolled trousers, why not applaud Rosie as she rolls up her sleeves?

Natural History

The Rufous hummingbird builds her nest
of moss and spider webs and lichen.
I held one once—smaller than my palm,
but sturdy. I would have told Mrs. Jeffers,
from Court Street, if in those days of constant flights
between California and Virginia I'd wandered
into that Oakland museum. Any chance
I could, I'd leave my rented house in Lynchburg.
I hated the feeling of stuckness that old city's humidity
implied. You need to stop running away so much,
Mrs. Jeffers would say when my visits were over
and I leaned down to hug her. Why her words
come to me, the woman dead for the better part
of this new century, while I think of that
nest of web and lichen, I cannot rightly say.
She had once known my mother's parents.
The whole lot of them, even then, in their twenties,
must already have been as old as God. They were
black—the kind name for them in those days
would have been Negroes—and the daily elections
called for between their safety and their sanity
must have torn even the strongest of them down.
Mr. Jeffers had been a laborer. The sort, I regret,
I don't remember. He sat on their front porch
all day, near his oxygen tank, waving occasionally
to passing Buicks and Fords, praising the black

walnut that shaded their yard. She would leave
the porch sometimes to prepare their meals.
I still have her yeast roll recipe. The best
I've ever tried. Mostly, though, the same Virginian
breeze that encouraged Thomas Jefferson's
tomatoes passed warmly through their porch eaves
while we listened to the swing chains, and no one
talked or moved too much at all. Little had changed
in that house since 1952. I guess it's no surprise
they'd come to mind when I think of that cup
of spider webs and moss, made softer by the feathers
of some long-gone bird. She used to say, I like it
right here where I am. In my little house. Here,
with him. I thought her small-minded. In the winter,
I didn't visit very often. Their house was closed up
and overheated. Everything smelled of chemical
mothballs. She had plastic wrappers on the sofas
and chairs. Everyone must have once
held someone as old and small and precious as this.

In my first book, *What to Eat, What to Drink, What to Leave for Poison*, there were two poems I almost took out. They felt too personal for a book of almost entirely persona, or what I call persona-ish, poems. They felt too confessional and raw. The me at the center of these more confessional poems did stupid things that shamed me, and this is another reason why I was tempted to remove them from the manuscript. The poems stayed in though. I figured that the fifty other poems in the collection would overshadow the two I was less certain about. This didn't happen. Instead, one of the two poems, "Cleaning," has since become one of my most frequently anthologized poems. I see the other making the rounds often as well. This taught me early that other people's taste in my poetry will not necessarily be the same as my own. It also taught me that when I feel like I am taking an emotional or revelatory risk in a poem, a risk that I'm hesitant to make in public, maybe that's exactly the direction a poem needs to go. Maybe other readers will respond to my vulnerability even if I am never able to feel particularly comfortable with my revelations myself.

Fast-forward to my fourth collection, *Trophic Cascade*. The poem "Natural History" shares the kind of energy I felt when I was writing "Cleaning." This might be because both poems have references to tomatoes and, though the town isn't named in "Cleaning," they are both about what I still carry with me from my family's time in Lynchburg, Virginia. About *thoughts* I still carry with me. The tangible artifacts and people connected to my family's life there have all been, in various ways, tossed away. In both poems, I am one of the primary tossers. The feeling of discomfort about knowing that I've thrown away something valuable is part of what drives both of these poems. This may be where the similarities end. There is plenty about the me in "Natural History" that still shames me. Plenty about the way I acted and the ideas I held that I wish I could do some other way. And yet, "Natural History" doesn't make me squirm when I read it the way that earlier poem still does.

One reason for this is likely that I have grown far more comfortable with revelations of my own foibles over time. Each new decade of my life has required me to laugh at myself a little longer and harder and more compassionately. Also, I think that I am less self-centered now than I was when I wrote that other poem. I don't need a poem to be either entirely about someone else (persona) or entirely about me. This dichotomy is a simplification of both what persona is and can be and what personal poems are and can be, but the rich potential of the wiggle room between these two extremes has also grown on me over time. This, again, is possibly the result of a few more years of living in the world with other people. And so "Natural History" is about me but also really isn't about me at all. It's about American history and tomatoes and hummingbirds and a sweet little old Black lady who tried to show me what grounded love looks like, even though it took me years to absorb the lesson. I like this poem because it is more expansive, both in terms of length and in terms of breadth. I feel like this poem includes *more* of me than the one that seems to be too much about me. The me I am in "Natural History" occupies far more geographies and bodies and histories, making her a more honest image of who I know myself to be.

Another thing I love about "Natural History": I get to use the word *rufous,* which is a funny-sounding word and tickles me. Later down the page, I get to crack something like a joke. That "older than God" line still makes me giggle when I read the poem out loud. It's way more bearable to write a poem, even a poem full of lots of serious content, as "Natural History" is, when I can find things in the world that help me laugh. Some of the line breaks in this poem make me smile. The chance to tease Thomas Jefferson still makes me smile, too. The world is broken in so many ways, and we are the ones doing most of the breaking, but also there are little cracks through which we can filter joy. Everything doesn't have to be so darned serious all the time. I love the ways that writing "Natural History" offered me pathways to beauty and humor and lightness and love.

The Theft Outright

after Frost

We were the land's before we were.

Or the land was ours before you were the land.
Or this land was our land, it was not your land.

We were the land before we were people,
loamy roamers rising, so the stories go,
or formed of clay, spit into with breath reeking soul—

What's America, but the legend of Rock 'n' Roll?

Red rocks, blood clots bearing boys, blood sands,
swimming being from women's hands, we originate,
originally, spontaneous as hemorrhage.

Un-possessing of what we still are possessed by,
possessed by what we now no more possess.

We were the land before we were people,
dreamy sunbeams where sun don't shine, so the stories go,
or pulled up a hole, clawing past ants and roots—

Dineh in documentaries scoff DNA evidence off.
They landed late, but canyons spoke them home.
Nomadic Turkish horse tribes they don't know.

What's America, but the legend of Stop 'n' Go?

Could be cousins, left on the land bridge,
contrary to popular belief, that was a two-way toll.
In any case we'd claim them, give them some place to stay.

Such as we were we gave most things outright
(the deed of the theft was many deeds and leases and claim stakes
and tenure disputes and moved plat markers stolen still today . . .)

We were the land before we were a people,
earthdivers, her darling mudpuppies, so the stories go,
or emerging, fully forming from flesh of earth—

The land, not the least vaguely, realizing in all four directions,
still storied, art-filled, fully enhanced.
Such as she is, such as she wills us to become.

GHOST ON THE SHELF

My drive as a teacher, writer, and human is to recognize both the history and presence of Native America and to speak to Native audiences in my work. Doing both is a contortionist trick. I perform this trick in "The Theft Outright," a poem that has made its way into several anthologies.

For years, I supported my writing life by teaching college during a time when Native American literature remained held to the margins and Native authors rarely made a booklist in American literature. Assigning Native-authored poetry was even more rare in a creative writing course. I assigned Native writers' books in every course. As required, I taught from the American literary canon, along with Greek drama, Shakespeare, and other dramatic works. My approach often focused on the view of Indigenous North America through

Euro-American authors' eyes—but prefaced by Native-authored writing. My experiment had mixed results. One student evaluation still stings: *I don't know why I had to read about a gay feather dancer.*

I persisted and carried both writing and literature students to some understanding or appreciation of an Indigenous worldview and the anti-image the literary canon produced. All along I marveled at American writers' view of "The Indian"—it was nothing familiar to me, an enrolled member of a tribe. To me "The Indian" was a literary ghost that I wanted to dispel, exorcise, or reveal for what it represented about a kind of haunting of the racial American literary conscience. But there was also a spirit there and, as an Ojibwe person, I wanted to feed it, ask it what it needed, and say it could move on.

When I stopped teaching undergraduates full-time, a colleague remarked *at least you don't have to suffer all the terrible student poetry.* I don't remember how I reacted outwardly, but I thought to myself, *suffered?* It's true that not all poems make it off the ground, but I've never suffered a bad first draft—it's raw material and usually needs to be built, not torn apart. And then there's always a moment of lift in a student writing workshop—when a poem, once a rickety contraption, is properly constructed and takes off on its first flight. I live for those moments as a teacher. Don't get me wrong, there were many grounded poems or those stripped for parts, but I laugh at the idea of suffering another's work. In fact, I get a lot of energy from mentoring students and I thank them for giving me the idea for "The Theft Outright" and other poems that are in many ways my lecture notes in lyric language.

At some point in my career of teaching creative writing and literature, I decided I would spend a year writing along with my students. I don't mean that I would write in class during their exercises, but that I would write in response to what we were reading together. Eventually, I decided I would write a book meant for students, and *National Monuments* was published in 2008 by Michigan State University Press. In this book, among other things, I confronted the ghosts in the American literary canon through my poems that spoke back to "great poems" that haunted me, horrified me, angered me, and sometimes amused me. Sometimes, as I had assigned my students, I wrote a parody or imitation using the structures of a famous poem. One such poem is "The Theft Outright," written in response to "The Gift Outright," the poem made famous when Robert Frost read it at President John F. Kennedy's inauguration.

That my poem "The Theft Outright" has regularly been anthologized sometimes surprises me. It sounds like Frost, not much like me, after all. It is accessible, too. That's a bit of an ouch—many of my poems move in mysterious ways—sometimes meant to tease. I don't think this poem represents my style at all—but perhaps it represents my substance.

Perhaps "The Theft Outright" has been anthologized because it directly talks back to the literary canon. It is a useful poem to teach and can be paired with Frost's poem, a twofer. It might also be chosen to illustrate a sort of Gen X of Native American poetry: the few writers who published their first books in the 1990s are not part of the Native American Literary Renaissance of the 1970s and early 1980s, and not considered along with the current crop of stellar poets first published since about 2010. If an anthologist is organizing chronologically and looking for a poet born in the 1960s, there are only a handful of well-published Native American poets from our generation—and there's my poem, already placed in context of the canon, a neat fit.

Writing at the end of the last century, we had little hope of a large Native audience for our poetry. Yet we write from an Indigenous or tribal sensibility. We didn't want to lose some of our readers for the sake of others—but we just had to write to people like ourselves. We had to do the contortionist's trick. I wrote "The Theft Outright" to work both as a kind of ironic imitation of Frost's poem and as a poem that Native audiences would understand on other levels. Because I wouldn't explain what I call "Easter Eggs for NDNs" and what the late Anishinaabe poet Jim Northrup called "Shinob Detectors" when I wrote "The Theft Outright," I won't do so now. Suffice it to say that some images that seem surreal are very real to members of some tribes. In writing "The Theft Outright" I contorted my poetic sensibility so that the poem would be understood by one group as a literary reference, but as a kind of landscape-specific manifesto on Indigenous land tenure by others. It's like tucking your head under your arm and walking forward—hard to do but it gets you going in one direction while seeing where you've been.

Frost wasn't supposed to read "The Gift Outright" for JFK. He had written another, much longer poem. The snow glare made it hard for Frost to see his intended poem, so he recited a much shorter one he knew by heart. He read less than half of what he had intended. Ironically, my poem "The Theft Outright" was published in the UK in an important anthology of American literature, and I was thrilled until I opened the book and saw that they had included only the first part of the poem. I heard Frost's ghost snicker.

For all my resistance to the literary canon, I am trained in American poetry and will never stop hearing Frost, Whitman, Williams, no matter how troubling their views of "The Indian" are to me. I can hear the power of Frost's poem as music and voice while I reject his meaning and his view that this land was devoid of culture and there for the taking, "unstoried" and "artless" and "unenhanced"—a gift outright. A gift from whom? Not us.

Frost's poem is meant to raise patriotic sentiments, but I hear a mean spirit in Frost's words, a denigration of my ancestors and relatives. When that mean spirit vexed me, when that ghost sat on the shelf demanding to be taught, I did what I was supposed to do with an unwelcome spirit: I fed it, asked it what it needed, and said with my revision: budge over in the canon and move on. Majaan!

Haunt Me

for my father

I am the archaeologist. I sift the shards of you: cufflinks, passport photos,

a button from the March on Washington with a black hand shaking

a white hand, letters in Spanish, your birth certificate from a town high

in the mountains. I cup your silence, and the silence melts like ice in a cup.

I search for you in two yellow Kodak boxes marked *Puerto Rico,*

Noche Buena, Diciembre 1968. In the 8-millimeter silence the Espadas

gather, elders born before the Spanish-American War, my grandfather

on crutches after fracturing his fossil hip, his blind brother on a cane.

You greet the elders and they call you *Tato,* the name they call you there.

Uncles and cousins sing in a chorus of tongues without sound, vibration

of guitar strings stilled by an unseen hand, maracas shaking empty

of seeds. The camera wobbles from the singers to the television

and the astronauts sending pictures of the moon back to earth.

Down by the river, women still pound laundry on the rocks.

I am eleven again, a boy from the faraway city of ice that felled

my grandfather, startled after the blind man with the cane stroked my face with his hand dry as straw, crying out *Bendito.* At the table,

I hear only the silence that rises like the river in my big ears.

You sit next to me, clowning for the camera, tugging the lapels

on your jacket, slicking back your black hair, brown skin darker

from days in the sun. You slide your arm around my shoulder,

your good right arm, your pitching arm, and my moon face radiates,

and the mountain song of my uncles and cousins plays in my head.

Watching you now, my face stings as it stung when my blind great-uncle

brushed my cheekbones, searching for his own face. When you died,

Tato, I took a razor to the movie looping in my head, cutting the scenes

where you curled an arm around my shoulder, all the times you would

squeeze the silence out of me so I could hear the cries and songs again.

When you died, I heard only the silences between us, the shouts belling

the air before the phone went dead, all the words melting like ice in a cup.

That way I could set my jaw and take my mother's hand at the mortuary,

greet the elders in my suit and tie at the memorial, say all the right words.

Yet, my face stings at last. I rewind and watch your arm drape across

my shoulder, over and over. A year ago, you pressed a Kodak slide

of my grandfather into my hand and said: *Next time, stay longer.*

Now, in the silence that is never silent, I push the chair away

from the table and say to you: *Sit down. Tell me everything. Haunt me.*

About "Haunt Me"

This poem speaks to what is essential in me: 1) My father and his death; 2) Puerto Rico and my first experience on the island.

Francisco Luis (Frank) Espada was born in the mountain town of Utuado, Puerto Rico, in 1930 and died in Pacifica, California, in 2014. He was a civil rights activist, a grassroots organizer, and a leader—some would say *the* leader—of the Puerto Rican community in New York during the 1960s and early 1970s. He was also a documentary photographer, the creator of the Puerto Rican Diaspora Documentary Project, a photo-documentary of the migration. He had more than forty solo exhibitions. His work has been collected in the Smithsonian Museum of American History, the Smithsonian Museum of American Art, the National Portrait Gallery, and the Library of Congress. He was a formidable figure; in another poem I called him "the tallest Puerto Rican in New York," who could "crack the walls with the rumble of his voice." He was a major influence, politically and poetically.

When he died in February 2014, I realized that I would have to write something to say at his memorial in Brooklyn. I sequestered myself in Craftsbury, Vermont, up in the "Northeast Kingdom," for a week to write an elegy. Ultimately, I ended up writing ten. This was the last poem I wrote for the cycle. Though I read another poem at the memorial—a laudatory piece more suited to the occasion—I always considered this poem to be most complex and accomplished of the ten, perhaps because it was the tenth shot at cracking my emotional armor. I finished the poem after the memorial; it has never been anthologized.

After my father's death, my mother sent along a veritable avalanche of miscellany from his life. Thus, I engaged in a ceremony familiar to almost anyone who has ever lost a parent: the ceremony of sorting through the junk. As so often happens, I found a treasure in the trash: two Super 8 silent "home movies," burned to DVD, documenting our pilgrimage to Puerto Rico for "Noche Buena," or Christmas Eve, in December of 1968. There was my father, still alive, thirty-eight years old, his hair still black. And there I was, pudgy and sweaty, an eleven-year-old fireplug from the projects of East New York in Brooklyn, visiting Puerto Rico for the first time, utterly bewildered by the living kinship network that embraced me and stretched back to the nineteenth century. (My grandfather and his brothers had been born before the Spanish-American War of 1898, when the United States took Puerto Rico from Spain, keeping the island as a colonized territory ever since.) Watching from the heights of the year 2014, I was quite unprepared to witness my father's spontaneous gesture of affection, putting his arm around my shoulder at the table, the way it lit me up.

And I broke.

I came to realize that I had been repressing grief in the name of efficiency, keeping my emotional turbulence at a distance so I could deal with the business of death, from the mortuary to the memorial, consoling my mother, saying "all the right words." Keeping my father at arm's length after death meant remembering only the "silences between us" and forgetting the arm around the shoulder. I had not yet allowed myself to cry. These contradictions made their way into the poem, so this elegy became more than the expected lamentation of loss or idealized remembrance. With the grief came guilt, vulnerability, and acknowledgment of tension in the history between us.

There was something more, manifested at the end of the poem: the recognition that I now had a relationship with a dead man—and that I could keep him alive, somehow, if I could keep him talking. In life, he wanted to talk; as the poem says, a year before his death, he virtually pleaded with me: "Next time, stay longer." And I never saw him again.

I had not only a responsibility to my father, but a responsibility to my poetry. To write well of grief, such that I could recognize the features of its face and others could too, thereby finding the consolation in my poems that I could not, I would have to welcome that grief to sit at my elbow. Most people swat the ghosts away. I feel an obligation to beckon them in and bid them stay. To be haunted is the only way I can write an elegy worthy of the dead, making the abstract "grief" concrete.

And here I should issue a disclaimer: I do not subscribe to the traditional notions of ghosts or hauntings. We are much closer to Hell on earth than Halloween. Yet, when my wife and I, staying by ourselves in an eighteenth-century Rhode Island house, awoke and came downstairs to find a chair moved away from the dining room table, as if for a guest to sit, that became the chair I push away from the table for my father at the end of the poem. "Haunt me," I say. And he does.

Tarfia Faizullah

Great Material

There were the blue-tied garbage bags
bulging with her dresses. Then, the buzz
of junebugs on nights I sat on the roof alone
and asked where my sister was until I felt stupid

and stopped. What do you say to the dead?
How can we rejoin them when we fall apart
in the safety net below? Does she know
her friends Lauren and Cameron played

house after she died, set a place for her
at a play dinner table? As though she
might stop by for a few bites of air
from empty plates with spoons empty

of her short seven years on this planet . . .
it unbottles me, how precisely they lamented
her. *What great material,* the conference
well-wisher said. *Can't wait to read that poem.*

Here it is then, now. The crinkle of your laughter.
The beetles pouring into your eyes as we toast you.

On "Great Material"

My sister Tangia died when I was twelve, and she was seven. I'm not sure if I would be a writer without her death. For what felt like a long time, I was racked with a grief that was both inconsolable and, as grief is, self-centered. I withdrew into the solace of my notebook, for how many years, and at what frequency, I cannot say exactly.

I also don't remember when, or how, I finally began to rejoin the world, as it were, but I did. I began to come alive again to the experiences of others. I wondered how losing my sister had affected others, including her classmates. They, too, were all so young at the time; for many of them, it was their first experience of loss, at least outside of an elderly grandparent or pet. There is a reason that so many people wince when they hear how young my sister was when she died; the death of a child is not just a tragedy, it makes us feel helpless, as does any injustice.

I couldn't stop wondering about Tangia's classmates' experience with her death. One night, thanks to both the uncanniness of social media and a sudden surge of spontaneity, I worked up the nerve to send a message to one of her former classmates, Cameron, and ask her. Cameron shared that she and Tangia's best friend, Lauren, continued to set a place for her when they played house. The idea of two young girls so perfectly observing and ritualizing grief is so moving to me, even now, so many years after the writing and publishing of this poem. That they grieved together—shouldered each other's shared loss—is all the more affecting.

A few months later, at a writers' conference, I was recounting the experience of speaking to Cameron to a few folks. "What great material for a poem!" enthusiastically responded a writer I had just met. I found that response so off-putting. I couldn't stop thinking about it, and wrestled with my own reaction as well. I was annoyed, but what was my problem? Hadn't she meant to be complimentary, and supportive? Except that I wasn't sure if I wanted to think about tragedy, in my life or in another's, as "great material"—something about that position seemed exploitative, or fetishizing, or vampiric, or something, even if understandable.

In the end, as you can see in the poem itself, I eventually succumbed to writing the scene of two little girls setting a place for a dead friend at a pretend dinner. Perhaps pettily, I also included the exchange with the conference goer; I didn't want to ignore the troubling questions the encounter stirred up. I decided to use that moment to break the walls of the poem, and therefore of the room, in which the younger versions of Lauren and Cameron are still innocently dining on air with my sister's absence. Outside of those walls is the larger, clumsier world, where questions about appropriation and exploitation must be reckoned with, alongside those regarding personal loss, and grief.

I have not said anything about the poem closing and opening with insects: junebugs, in the first stanza, and beetles, in the last. There is not much to say, except that it is a fact.

Jennifer Elise Foerster

The Last Kingdom

Three days before the hurricane
a woman in white is hauling milk.

The beach wails.
She is swinging her pail.

I am sleeping in a tent of car parts, quilts
when the woman passes through the heavy felt door.

If your dream were to wash over the village, she says.
We listen—seagulls resisting the shore.

Hermit crabs scuttle under tin.
The children hitch their sails in.

Later that night from the compound walls
I see her hitchhiking the stars' tar road—

black dress, black boots, black bonnet,
a moon-faced baby in a basket.

. . .

      Thus, alone, I have conceived.

A tent dweller moved to the earth's edge,
I bathe in acidic waves.

Everyone in the village
watches at the cliff the tidal wave
breach, roll across the sky.

They are feasting on cold
fried chicken, champagne—
        I have no dancing dress for the picnic.

The king dozes in his gravelly castle.
The band plays its tired refrain.

Men, drunk on loosened wind
raise their cups to mechanical dolphins
tearing through the sheet-metal sea.

In the shadow of petrels'
snowy specters, drifting monuments
crash and calve.

But I, as water under wind does,
I tear my hair,
scalp the sand—

the sun, eclipsed by dark contractions
turns its disc to night—

fish like bright coins
flip from my hand.

. . .

        Waking, I find I am alone in the kingdom.

The moon lays upon me
its phosphorescent veil.

The floating world—luciferous:
bleached coral coliseum,
a mermaid's molten gown—

she turns her widening wheels,
spills her pail of glacial milk.

I could almost swim forever
to her beat of frozen bells.

But a sheet of water
doesn't travel with the wave.

And the morning like a tender body
slides out of silt:

I press against its damp
rough surface, an ear.

As with most of my poems, the source for "The Last Kingdom" is my prismatic and chaotic dream world. This underside of my consciousness is so tumultuous that, while it generates wild and wonderous insights, sensations, and fragments of experience, it seems impossible to funnel any of this into language, let alone meaningful language. This is why I turn to poetry, because poetry is the only place I feel I have any chance of catching these fleeting colors and forms. Once caught, the essence may still slip away. But sometimes it stays and the poem becomes its vessel, a kaleidoscope I can keep turning to study its series of innate designs.

What I continue to like about "The Last Kingdom" is how unchaotic it turned out to be despite its origin in the dream world. While I revised this poem many times for its lineation, rhythms, sonics, and images, it became what it is because of something I can't ultimately command or articulate. Poetry is forever eluding our best efforts at reasoning and rules. It will evade our control according to its own whims.

If poetry is such an elusive being (or ghost), why even bother to apply our techniques and structures of language? Because the poem won't make itself on its own. We need rules and forms to craft a language with which to hold the poetry we are drawn to translate. I say "translate" instead of "create" because poetry is a language of translation: translation of the invisible and ineffable. This doesn't mean our writing isn't also an act of creation. The question I hold, as a poet who holds these beliefs about poetry, is, how can I engage my creativity toward translating something invisible and ineffable *without* translating it out of or away from itself? The writing of "The Last Kingdom" did not stifle the dreaming from whence it came. This is why the poem still speaks to me.

The poem began with an inciting image, the clearest of a set of murky images I awoke with one day: a woman on a beach with a pail at the advent of a storm. Following this were a few images each identifiable by a noun: milk, a tent, an iceberg, and a king. Now I had enough to begin. A few intriguing images or objects can be a sturdy foundation for any poem, especially if these images or objects are unusual and unlike one another. The imagination has no choice but to wake up when you ask: What does milk have to do with an iceberg? A storm with a tent? A king with a beach?

Once I had a primary constellation of characters, objects, and images, the next "rules" I applied to the creative process were those of sound, because I wanted the poem to be musical. The narratives suggested by the image constellation may not yet make sense, but creating a musicality could invite a different kind of sense to the scene. Applying a sonic structure meant several actions: controlling the lineation to manipulate meter, pacing, and rhythm; and being elective in diction to enable sonic effects such as assonance, alliteration, or slant rhymes.

I wanted only the suggestion of meter and rhyme, just enough to give the poem a roundedness, but as the nature of the poem was mysterious, too much meter and rhyme might flatten out the poem's strangeness. The rhyming words are closer together in the first section but aren't adherent to a strict rhyme scheme; the second section keeps its end-rhymes farther apart (*champagne, refrain, sand, hand*); the third section has even fewer end-rhymes but is held together by slant or internal rhymes (*kingdom* and *coliseum; veil, pail, bells*) and by a generous scattering of alliterations. Further, while I used couplets to help arrange the interplay of short and long sentences and the presentation of imagery, I departed from this form at moments to give space for the more disorderly and emotional energy that is part of the poem's origin.

By composing this poem according to sound, I discovered more of the poem's imaginative material. Coming up with a word to rhyme with *champagne* inspired the idea of a band playing a refrain, which introduced a kind of circular madness to the scenario. "Cold fried chicken [and] champagne" came from a conversation with a friend about their favorite meal—something I'd then written in my notebook because I liked how it sounded. I often mine my notebook for things that resonate with poems I'm working on, and the frivolous feast of a lazy king seemed the right home for this phrase.

I was also reading W.B. Yeats at the time while toiling over (which I continue to do) our climate crisis. The Emperor of Yeats's "Byzantium" felt much like my poem's drunken kingsmen, so I made them raise their cups to my version of "that dolphin-torn, that gong-tormented sea."

The heart of the inciting image was for me a solitary woman on the beach who knew what was coming when the rulers of the world refused to see. She was intentional with that pail; she was someone who worked, humbly, and carried the secrets. She became, in my reconstruction of the dream material, the village seer. I often think I dream hurricanes before they happen. But hurricanes are always happening. I am not the village seer, just a poet.

The "I" in this poem is the poet—the person seeing this seer and the outside witness to the unseeing party. She is the dreamer who wakes up alone with the images, who has conceived of something she must care for but doesn't know how to, and who knows only how to *listen* for what meaning the mystery may reveal. This is the role of the poet in the life of poetry. Sometimes, "fish like bright coins / flip from my hand"—what luck! And then they slip away.

The Garden Shukkei-en

By way of a vanished bridge we cross this river
as a cloud of lifted snow would ascend a mountain.

She has always been afraid to come here.

It is the river she most
remembers, the living
and the dead both crying for help.

A world that allowed neither tears nor lamentation.

The *matsu* trees brush her hair as she passes
beneath them, as do the shining strands of barbed wire.

Where this lake is, there was a lake,
where these black pine grow, there grew black pine.

Where there is no teahouse I see a wooden teahouse
and the corpses of those who slept in it.

On the opposite bank of the Ota, a weeping willow
etches its memory of their faces into the water.

Where light touches the face, the character for heart is written.

She strokes a burnt trunk wrapped in straw:
I was weak and my skin hung from my fingertips like cloth.

Do you think for a moment we were human beings to them?

She comes to the stone angel holding paper cranes.
Not an angel, but a woman where she once had been,

who walks through the garden Shukkei-en
calling the carp to the surface by clapping her hands.

Do Americans think of us?

So she began as we squatted over the toilets:
If you want, I'll tell you, but nothing I say will be enough.

We tried to dress our burns with vegetable oil.

Her hair is the white froth of rice rising up kettlesides, her mind also.
In the postwar years she thought deeply about how to live.

The common greeting *dozo-yiroshku* is please take care of me.
All *hibakusha* still alive were children then.

A cemetery seen from the air is a child's city.

I don't like this particular red flower because
it reminds me of a woman's brain crushed under a roof.

Perhaps my language is too precise, and therefore difficult to understand?

We have not, all these years, felt what you call happiness.
But at times, with good fortune, we experience something close.
As our life resembles life, and this garden the garden.
And in the silence surrounding what happened to us

it is the bell to awaken God that we've heard ringing.

ON THE GARDEN SHUKKEI-EN

Most of my poems are lyric embodiments of memory or experience, although some few seem to rise out of nowhere, untethered to my own life. "The Garden Shukkei-en" is an inscription, in lyric form, of a conversation that took place in a historic garden in the city of Hiroshima. In the summer of 1983, the Asian Writers Congress convened to discuss the theme of writing "Literature Under the Nuclear Cloud." Two poets were invited from each nation possessing nuclear weapons at that time: the United States, Russia, the United Kingdom, France, China, and also Israel, which has not yet acknowledged its nuclear forces. Two poets were also invited from the Republic of South Africa, which briefly developed nuclear weapons but has since relinquished them. Galway Kinnell and I were the invited poets from the United States.

We were to travel by train to Hiroshima and Nagasaki, where we would give readings, attend receptions, participate in panel discussions, and informally discuss the threat of nuclear war and its impress upon the poetic imagination. We visited the epicenters of the destructive force of the weapons, the peace parks and monuments, and walked through collections of objects preserved from the rubble: bottle caps embedded in molten bottle glass, clothing stained with the shadows of flesh, melted coins, a burnt tricycle, sewing needles fused together, the scraps of a child's summer uniform. We placed wreaths at the cenotaphs and were given bouquets of folded paper cranes. Just yesterday and by coincidence, I opened the box where the cranes have been kept for decades. They are intact, almost forty years later.

We also spoke with survivors, who told their stories, as they had thousands of times since 1945. The testimonies were preceded by apologies for Japanese aggression in the Pacific during the war. Then they began: *at 8:15 a.m. on August 6 at 11:02 a.m. on August 9.* A flash of light they called the *pika.* A hissing sound. Silence. I will not write the rest.

At this time, it had been thirty-eight years since the bombings. The survivors offering their memories would have mostly been children in

1945. When I asked them what they remembered of their lives before that August, they said they did not remember, or no longer did, and seemed somewhat confused by the question.

It was announced that the visiting poets would be taken to Sentei Garden (Shukkei-en) in the afternoon, a short walk from the cenotaph.

Photo by Carolyn Forché

Recently, I read the testimony of Kasumi Miyai, who had been working in a munitions factory in the summer of 1945 while attending school. She remembered being pinned under the weight of beams, and then fleeing, and somehow arriving at Shukkei-en, where burned "sleepwalkers" had taken refuge, sitting "quietly in the rain as if they were just waiting for time to pass." But Kasumi Miyai would not offer her testimony until the twenty-first century. Another woman was among us then, who was, she said, a child at the time of the bombings, but she did not give her age. When she heard that the poets would visit the garden, she asked to come with us. To our hosts, this was welcome news, and momentous. The woman had been in the garden Shukkei-en that terrible morning, and believed herself to have been saved by the intervention of a grove of trees. In all the years since, she had not brought herself to return there, despite that the damaged garden had been restored. However, if the poets were going, she wished to accompany them. I knew that I had to walk beside her, and was given the opportunity to do so, as one of the few women in the delegation, and among the youngest. A shy, bilingual high school girl served as our interpreter, and found herself at a loss for words only a few times.

"The Garden Shukkei-en" is a dialogic poem of narrator and survivor. I wrote it as sparely as I could, and as faithfully to its occasion. All phrases in the survivor's voice were transcribed into a notebook soon after we left the garden. I wrote them from the same impulse and in the same manner as I recorded the words of my paternal grandmother, Anna, who appeared in my early poems, and those of Elie, my wardmate in the hospital *Hôtel-Dieu,* who became the interlocutor in the title poem of *The Angel of History,* the volume in which "The Garden Shukkei-en" appears.

I have always written down the words of older women. I have always been drawn to them. What I remember of that garden visit were the men walking on the path ahead of us, always ahead, and the light on the still lake, the reflection of an arched bridge in the water, the survivor's silver hair gathered into a bun, the years in her eyes, and the way she seemed as much to talk to herself as to me. She was, like other survivors, willing to endure living through her memories again if it might make some small difference in the world, especially if it might turn the world away from nuclear weapons. God, after all, must have been asleep in 1945. It is time to wake up. The comparison of a cemetery seen from the air to a child's city is mine; the red flower compared to *a woman's brain crushed under a roof* is hers. The question *Do Americans think of us?* was also hers, and I could not offer her an answer.

Anaberto FaceTimes with His Mother

He sits in Manhattan, she stands
in Michoacán, in the kitchen he abandoned
every day of his youth. How sluggish
her cooking, her hand always heavy on

the salt. Each pot a story running out
of breath long before the finish. He hides
his palates from her—behind him a table
like a gem display: croquettes of steaming

amber, rubies over salad, a string
of onion pearls flung into the omelet.
His prowess in the culinary arts
a desire he fulfills one thousand

meals apart from his beloved mother,
who inadvertently conspired to dull his senses.
Nonetheless he loves her, won't offend her
by admitting to the craft he practices

in New York—joy denied in México.
How thin my son without my stews, she fears,
how lonely and neglected he must feel
without a woman in this place he shares

with another boy, another orphan
from God-knows-where. "How is he, anyway?"
she asks, and then a second face appears,
pretty and golden as her son's. The young

man smiles, a coy expression that suggests
he isn't going hungry either. He seems quite
content in the country that her son had
fled to, she suspected, for God-knows-what.

———

"Anaberto FaceTimes with His Mother" is an unusual poem for me for the following reasons: it includes a mention of technology (which is rare in my poetry), it shifts point of view from the son to the mother (which I've not done before), and it is not explicit about what the poem is *also* about. Astute readers will note that Anaberto's cooking is not the only thing he's hiding from his mother and that she's in fact quite clueless about her son's private life.

I made these choices because I wanted to situate the poem in a very contemporary setting while reminding readers that some things don't change, like the fact that young people (even now that conversations about sexuality and gender identity are in the public discourse) have to come to terms with who they are at their own pace. Each journey is unique and individual, and for some, staying in the closet is still a stage on that journey, for various reasons.

In Anaberto's case, I wanted to be clear that the mother is not the villain, and that Anaberto is protecting her from his truths, out of respect and because he loves her. This was something I experienced as a young Mexican boy who knew he was gay but was not ready to reveal that to the family because of the uncertainties: Would my father get angry? Would my mother be hurt? Would they still love me? Perhaps Anaberto will come out to his mother when he's older, but at the moment he's in college, in a new country, expressing his new freedoms and trying to find his footing in the world. He needed to venture out on his own because at home, things "conspired to dull his senses."

The shifting point of view was my nod to the FaceTime feature. In the old days, it was much easier to conceal things through letters and phone calls, but with FaceTime, reality is literally looking at you in the face, yet that doesn't necessarily mean you know what you're looking at. The mother and son are emotionally connected through technology, but a few secrets are still keeping them apart. For the duration of the exchange over FaceTime, however, the mother's perspective and Anaberto's are equally valid, important, and true.

One final thing: I chose cooking as Anaberto's hidden talent because he comes from a culture similar to mine, in which it is expected that women perform that task because it is considered women's work. Interestingly enough, in my household it was my grandfather who did all the cooking. My grandmother, bless her heart, was a terrible cook. This was generally known to family members outside of our immediate household and no one ever batted an eye. So what? The man does the cooking in that house. I always wondered if the day would come when they would have the same level of acceptance or disinterest for the defiance of other gender norms. I like to think that as times changed, so did they. But even if they haven't, I was still able to find another place (like Anaberto) to be the person I wanted to be.

Why

you ask me
again—why
putting your tiny hand on
the not yet

unsheathed
bud on the
rhododendron,
and I see

I need to be sky
I need to be soil
there are no words
for why that I

can find fast
enough, why
you say at
the foot of the cherry's wide

blossomfall
is it dead now why
did it let go, *why,*
tossed out

into what appears
to be silence
when I say
let's run the

rain is starting—why
are we lost why did
we just leave
where we just

were why is
everything
so far behind
now as we go on I

see you think
when you reach
me again to ask
why when I say

are you coming now &

you say no,
I want to stay, I want
things to stay, I do
not want to come

away from things—what
is this we are
entering—me taking yr
hand now to speed

our going
as fast as we can in this suddenly
hard rain, yr
hand not letting go

of the rose pebble u found
feeling the first itching of
personal luck as
you now slowly

pocket it thinking
you have taken
with you a piece of
what u could not

leave behind. It is
why we went there
and left there.
It is your why.

for Samantha

This poem surprised me on many levels. It appears to be a small story, simple to tell, but in fact the story is not something that happened this way in "real life" at all. It was discovered—and the process of its discovery reminded me once again about the mysteries of composition in poetry, as everything in these dimeter quatrains gave rise to ways of discovering what poem, exactly, was trying to find its way through to my page. That is always a small heart-stopping miracle.

First of all the shortness of the line awakened the shortness of the spoken phrases—so the quick breaths, the feeling of urgent repeated questioning by a child, the needed fast answers the adult grasps to find—(leading me to make them both slightly out of breath, moving them from walking to running).

The small narrative of their journey did not appear at all at first—only three images. Sometimes freestanding images or objects tell a secret story which holds a poem before I find its arc or narrative. Plumbing those images is my way to finding that poem. Here, the rhododendron bud (pink, hard yet softening), fallen cherry blossom (tissue-soft, already moving towards decay), and the rose pebble (apparently unalterable, almost eternal in its mineral hardness, though the smoothness of the pebble is the result of the continual passage of deep time) created an image-cluster which suddenly held the entire poem out to me. But how to find that poem?

I looked at those three: they are the same size—perfect to be held in a small closed fist. They share color—a similar shade of pink. They unfold in three radically different temporalities—the cycle of the plant life—(unopened bud, finished blossom)—the long life of circular time, but brief duration, of the blossom on its arc—and the unfathomably long life of the mineral quartz pebble, ancient and from the depths of earth. The first is touched as if to help it open, as if its time corresponded to human time. The second enacts how quickly time takes away all beauty.

The third makes a promise which we mistake: it promises to never change again, to stop time and time's apparently destructive action.

The first is briefly touched by the hand of the child, the second held by its glance—revealing its appalling truth—the third is found by mind and hand and secreted away from the eye, the day, time, into the mind, the pocket, inwardness, memory. The child is awakened into a feeling of personal fate by the finding of the pebble—which replaces the other versions of time the walk has revealed. The truths about life, death, beauty, evanescence, about the indifference which lives alongside our one temporal journey in our shared universe, are taken in until they suddenly stop the child in her tracks and make her stutter her powerful no. That moment took me by surprise. At first I didn't know how to proceed from there.

The pocketing of the pebble, the awakening of a desire which will work to oppose those intuited truths—(time's decay, time's plan for us all)—were the next surprise. That impulse holds the bedrock human response to the intimation of not only mortality but also the indifference of nature and our outsideness in relation to it. This outsideness is also enacted formally in the poem by the layering ever-outward of successive possible speakers or narrators. The finding, the owning, the taking possession, the bringing inward—all these mimic in a gesture how that intimation entered the soul through the eye—though the hand weighs down what the eye saw and spirit intuited, freights it with grief, desire, the instinct towards ownership and brittle individuality. As for the rest—what I did was create the simplest story, a setting that provided the fullest opportunity to act out the overtones, meanings, and implications of those three objects.

First off, I put in the path, then their speeding up and slowing down on it, then their turning back. Near the end I added rain oncoming—to create hurry. At the very last draft I made the rain not hold off, but start during the poem—so they could not get ahead of it. I made the rain sudden and fast, which made the revelation need to speed up and become urgent. It had to be delivered in driving rain. I also made it possible for the "no"—(the refusal to go on into time, the intimation that going forward is only towards ruin, the terrible desire to not move further into mortality)—to rise up in the midst of an acoustic field (it is raining hard, there are many sounds into which the "no" and the "stay" are cast). Then, as if because of the rain, the voices intermingled in some places—(who is the child, who is the adult)—so that there is room as well for a third voice, the voice of the poet, who comes down and joins them in the rain ("what / is this we are / entering").

The why felt radically innocent—but also, the simplified force of the question, like a blade or a wedge, cracked open far wider and deeper questions: why anything exists at all, why we exist in time, why time keeps moving us away from an irrecoverable past—in other words the primordial "why?" We are out for a walk. We are exposed. The season is changing, blossoms fall and die. A fast-moving rainstorm is moving in. Why? The "why" keeps exerting its counterpressure, part

inquiry, part protest. But then, "there are no words / for why that I //
can find fast / enough."

Thus the poem reaches the limits of communication itself, and these
limits, like the limits of what can indeed be answered, are inseparable
from a naïve yet powerful resistance to giving up, to surrendering to
time, to the passage away from here towards not just displacement
itself but, yes (despite our "no"), towards death. Partly because of the
doubled perspectives of child and adult, with their to and fro literally
aligned with the turnings back and forth of short verse lines, the plu-
ral speakers come not simply to feeling loss but to feeling lost: "why /
are we lost . . ."

On the one hand the situation remains simple, a child and grand-
parent living in time. But the sense of lostness, of unknowability about
what we are "entering," makes it hard to separate the poem's occasion
and its why from an aggravating menace: this late in the Anthropo-
cene, how much of a prior natural world have we destroyed or pre-
vented from unsheathing itself into existence? How much temporal
change, dislocation, dispossession have we accelerated? Losing what
was once just behind us, the world we once inhabited—is there any-
thing we can take with us? In this way the poem finally reveals itself as
an Expulsion.

Hopefully the poem becomes a kind of rose pebble, something
made and not merely found, something to keep in the pocket of the
mind, or the spirit, or the numinous envelope which invests us like
a garment. A rose pebble. Something as lapidary as it is verbal. Some-
thing poised between mineral and mind. Some "thing" that may
become our reason for being and going. Not our answer but our living
out the fullness of the question.

User's Guide to Physical Debilitation

Should the painful condition of irreversible paralysis

last longer than forever or at least until

your death by bowling ball or illegal lawn dart,

you, or your beleaguered caregiver

stirring dark witches' brews of resentment

inside what had been her happy life,

should turn to page seven where you can learn,

assuming higher cognitive functions

were not pureed by your selfish misfortune,

how to leave the house for the first time in two years.

An important first step,

with apologies for the thoughtlessly thoughtless metaphor.

When not an outright impossibility

or form of neurological science fiction,

sexual congress will probably be one of three things:

an act of sadistic charity performed

by tourists in the kingdom of your tragedy;

by the curious, for whom you will be beguilingly blank canvas;

or someone blindly feeling their way

through an extended power outage

caused by summer storms you once thought romantic.

Page twelve instructs you how best

to be inspiring to Magnus next door

as he throws old Volkswagens into orbit

above Alberta. And to Betty

in her dark charm confiding a misery,

whatever it is, that to her seems equivalent to yours.

The curl of her hair that her finger knows

better and beyond what you will,

even in the hypothesis of heaven

when you sleep. This guide is intended

to prepare you for falling down

and declaring détente with gravity,

else you reach the inevitable end

of scaring small children by your presence alone.

Someone once said of crushing

helplessness: it is a good idea to avoid that.

We agree with that wisdom

but gleaming motorcycles are hard

to turn down or safely stop

at speeds which melt aluminum. Of special note

are sections regarding faith

healing, self-loathing, abstract hobbies

like theoretical spelunking and extreme atrophy,

and what to say to loved ones

who won't stop shrieking

at Christmas dinner. New to this edition

is an index of important terms

such as catheter, pain, blackout,

pathological deltoid obsession, escort service,

magnetic resonance imaging,

loss of friends due to superstitious fear,

and, of course, amputation

above the knee due to pernicious gangrene.

It is our hope that this guide

will be a valuable resource

during this long stretch of boredom and dread

and that it may be of some help,

however small, to cope with your new life

and the gradual, bittersweet loss

of every God damned thing you ever loved.

—

The germ of so many poems is desire, for a beloved other or a bygone time. To be, as Tomaž Šalamun wrote, a "hunter in the forest." I get that. I understand it. So many of my poems began that way. But "User's Guide to Physical Debilitation" wasn't steeped in loss or nostalgia; I'd just read a review of a collection of essays by the wonderful poet Lucia Perillo and my reaction changed, sentence by sentence, from indifference to bemusement to frustration. The reviewer marveled that Perillo could write about bird-watching on one page and making love with her husband on the next, as if her disability had made life a hellish sort of magic trick. I remember being insulted—for her. For myself. I went for an agitated stroll around my neighborhood and began, in my mind, to write this poem. The reviewer needed some kind of field guide to disability. A primer on the flesh. Retaliation rather than consolation.

After writing it, being kind of pleased by its venom, I tried reading it a few times and was struck by how often it failed to go over with audiences. To me, it was funny. But an uncomfortable hush would descend like a blackout curtain between us. A few might laugh, and I would love them for getting it. But most people were quiet. Unsure. Still.

When I was twelve years old, I broke my neck in a bicycle accident, paralyzing me from the neck down. That sentence is all fact but it doesn't move like a poem. Or feel like one. And I spent years avoiding my disability as a writer because I couldn't figure out a way to write that part of my life that wasn't terrible or mawkish or, maybe worst of all, dull. This wasn't the first time I wrote a poem about being disabled, but I feel like it gets close to something true about how it feels, at least to me.

But I rarely read the poem aloud. I share it here with you. Was it Twain who said that nothing is more serious than a joke? I don't know.

The Unbearable Heart

In the train an hour along the Sound, distant from the details of grief
I look up from the news toward the salt marshes
clumped beneath a snow we thought we would not see this year;
snow fallen twice this past week since Mother died, instantly, 10:35 p.m.,
broadsided by an Arab kid fleeing a car of white kids with baseball bats;
a snow only matched by my father's head as I reach to touch him
as I have never touched him. He wishes
he could see her once more, to say goodbye,
as Ted and I said goodbye to the body that was Mother's.
Grief comes in spasms: the smell of banana bread, I think of the rotting fruit
my sister and I tossed before Father came home from Yonkers General.
A flashlight. The flashlight she bought my youngest daughter
who always rummaged for one under Grandpa's side of the mattress.
The orange day lilies the florist sent to our apartment:
the lilies from the woods she brought to my wedding.

And when I told my six-year-old, Grandma died in the accident,
after tears and questions, she suggested, maybe now is a good time
to explain what the man has to do with babies.
So, I chose one perfect lily from that vase
and with the tip of a paring knife slit open the pistil
to trace the passage pollen makes to the egg cell—
the eggs I then slipped out and dotted on her fingertip, the greenish white
translucent as the air in this blizzard that cannot cool the unbearable heart.

As I write this, I still demand your attention, Mother.

And now that she's gone how do we find her—
especially my small daughters who will eventually recall their grandmother
not as a snapshot in the faults of the mind
but as the incense in their hair long after the reading of the Lotus Sutra.

⸺

How and what do we remember? I think in the West we privilege images as if those we recollect are souvenir snapshots. But a musician I know can recall sounds the way I remember, say, my sixth birthday cake, white with a Cinderella figure and pink coach. When my terrier lies on my chest, I recall the weight of my infant daughter. When I smelled plumeria in Central America, I recalled my grandmother's home in Maui. Our senses prompt recollection.

I think that sensory work is underutilized. For "The Unbearable Heart" I wanted to use smell and taste as indelible sensory images. I wanted to hold on to keen recollections from the days after my mother died. And, of course, to convey my grief.

But all these craft challenges did not enter my mind when I was sitting on a train that was heading north along the Long Island Sound. I was reading a newspaper when I looked out the window into the gray mist. During that awful time everything appeared tinged by her death. I scribbled in a kind of journal frame of mind: what was happening on that particular day and, especially, what I was thinking as I replayed what I'd learned about the car accident and, in the aftermath, what I'd told my small daughters. The six-year-old did not understand and, among other odd comments, she really did ask about babies. And I did use a flower to explain.

In hindsight, I think the italicized line where I suddenly address my mother, was meant to pull the speaker/reader back, for a moment. The way one might suddenly "speak" to a person who has died, then, as quickly, return from that netherworld to the awful mundane.

The closure returns to the theme of recollection and the belief that scent is the most powerful conveyer of memory. Especially for small children who may not retain visual images of their grandmother. Coupled with that scent is hearing the Lotus Sutra, commonly intoned at Buddhist funerals. I imagine the chant would be especially moving for a child.

Aside from the above, I also used my understanding of Japanese poetics. My penchant for lists (banana bread, flashlight, lilies) comes from my interest in the zuihitsu. Sei Shonagon's *Pillow Book* is filled with such lists, and although a list in and of itself is not Japanese, what I learned about the form derives from her models. Additionally, double meanings are prized in Japanese poetics and so I, too, love to play with words: *Sound/sound, unbearable heart/heat, faults.* Maybe *incense, Sutra/suture.*

Why is this poem never anthologized? With my enthusiastic nod, the book designer Yuko Uchikawa laid out the typography on two facing pages, flush right and flush left, so the poem resembled a heart. It was a striking artistic move, but I think the layout discouraged anthologists. Or perhaps the poem's importance is more personal, perhaps it is less moving for others. That's always possible.

katherine with the lazy eye. short. and not a good poet.

this morning, i heard you were found in your mcdonald's uniform.

i heard it while i was visiting a lake town, where empty
woodsy highways turn into waterside drives.

i'd forgotten my toothbrush and was brushing my teeth with one finger.
a friend who didn't know you said he'd heard it like this: *you know*
    katherine. short.

with a lazy eye. poet. not a very good one. yeah, well she died. the blue on that lake
isn't so frank. it fogs off into the horizon like styrofoam. the

picnic tables full of white people. i ask them where the coffee is. they say
    at meijer.

i wonder if you thought about getting out of detroit. when you read at the
    open mic
you'd point across the street at mcdonald's and tell us to come see you.

katherine with the lazy eye. short and not a good poet, i guess i almost cried.
i don't know why, because i didn't like you. this is the first i remembered
    your name.

i didn't like how you followed around a married man. that your poems sucked
and that i figured they were all about the married man.

that sometimes you reminded me of myself, boy crazy. that sometimes
i think people just don't tell me that i'm kind of, well . . . slow.

katherine with the lazy eye, short. and not a good poet.
i didn't like that your lazy eye was always

looking at me. that you called me by my name. i didn't
like you, since the first time i saw you at mcdonald's.

you had a mop. and you were letting some homeless dude
flirt with you. i wondered then, if you thought that was the best

you could do. i wondered then
if it was.

katherine with the lazy eye, short. and not a good poet.
you were too silly to wind up dead in an abandoned building.

i didn't like you because, what was i supposed to tell you. what.
don't let them look at you like that, katherine. don't let them get you alone.

katherine with the lazy eye, short. and not a good poet. what
was i supposed to say to you, you don't get to laugh like that,

like nothing's gonna get you. not everyone
will forgive the slow girl. katherine with

the fucked up eye, short. poetry sucked, musta knew better. i avoided you
in the hallway. i avoided you in lunch line. i avoided you in the lake.

i avoided you. my lazy eye. katherine with one hideous eye, shit.
poetry for boys again, you should have been immune. you were supposed

to be a cartoon. your body was supposed to be as twisted as
it was gonna get. short. and not a good poet. katherine with

no eye no more. i avoided you. hated it when you said my name. i really want to leave detroit. katherine with the lazy short.

not a good poet. and shit. somewhere someone has already asked *what was she like,* and a woman has brought out her wallet and said

this is her. this is my beautiful baby.

I don't think "The Katherine Poem" (as I've come to call it) is my *best* poem. But to date, it remains my most striking confessional poem. I wrote it in a poem-a-day project with a small group of friends in 2007, I believe. I wrote it quickly. I did not edit a lot. I think of it as a poem written in real time—written the way it happened, when and where it happened. It is the kind of poem that happens when you are reading and writing a lot. It has a built-in cadence that echoes the music in your head.

At heart in TKP is an admission that news of a young poet's death stirred guilt. The "friend who didn't know you" was one of my closest friends, Blair. For a long time, I was afraid to read it in public. But Blair thought it was good. So I brought it to a few open mics. Eventually, I included it in my first book, *allegiance.*

When I still visited public high schools as a writer, I went to Detroit International Academy, an all-girls school. I brought it with me. I never knew what to read from *allegiance,* since it was pretty dark. Funny, but only in its harsh, often sexual, imagery. I had to replace all the curse words. I had to be a little more upbeat.

On this day, I visited a class where my name was projected onto the wall. The room was lowlit. The image of my face stayed up while I read. I read a few poems I thought made the cut for the young girls in their smart-looking gray-and-black school uniforms. Some of the girls were attentive. A few were quiet. I read The Katherine Poem. "katherine with the lazy eye. short. and not a good poet," I started. They seemed to sit up. It struck them. Some of them audibly engaged during the read.

Ohh. Mnm. Heavy sigh.

One girl sat midrow, near the center of the room. She was big for her age. She let the uniform hang on her like a costume, clunky and oddly tucked. Thick black socks all the way to her knees. Big black shoes. It was a whole mood, and she knew it.

Afterward, we had Q&A. Yes, I liked to write in public. No, I didn't memorize my poems. Yes, when I was your age, I had a journal and someone snatched it and read one of my poems to the whole class and I thought I would die.

Then the girl with thick socks shot her hand straight up into the air.

I knew I was about to be mocked. I braced for it. She said:

"Can I ask you a question about the poem you read. About the girl who died."

"Okay," I said. "Sure."

"Did you feel better about yourself when you wrote that poem?"

I had prepared for it. But I was not prepared. I froze. She isolated so much of how I felt about the poem, about myself. Frankly, about writing in general.

She was mocking me. But her question was real.

"Yes." I think I said. To soften the sarcasm. "Yes, in the sense that writing always feels better."

Or maybe I said:

"No. Not really. Writing never really makes you feel better about whatever you're writing about. It just feels good to write."

Either way, I answered her poorly. Her question scared me. Maybe *she* scared me.

...

Early in Augustine's *Confessions,* he writes of the inescapable sin of wanting the world to revolve around himself. He writes:

Gradually I began to perceive where I was, and to want to express my needs to those who could fulfill them; but I could not express them, for the needs were inside me, and the other people outside; nor were they able with any of their senses to enter my soul. So I kicked and shouted; these were the few signs I could make that resembled my wishes, though they did not really resemble them.

This, which Augustine acknowledges as childishness, still clearly qualified as unholy for him. And similarly, there is a kind of temper tantrum at work in The Katherine Poem. An inability to control someone else's reaction to the world being the sole reason the speaker doesn't like them. In so many ways, the poem feels like a confession of my own immaturity. And so not only reminds me that I should be kinder in my approximations, but reminds me the reminder is necessary at all.

What I should have told Miss Socks is the nature of frustration does "not really resemble" the wishes of our holy selves. Thus, poem. Poems beautifully emulate the sound of our frustrated psyche in the face of its own temper tantrum.

And I should have told her the nature of confession is twofold. There is the cleansing nature. Be it to God, or self, or reader. As she smartly pointed out, it does make me—with all the irony intended—feel better about myself.

But there is something else. About time.

Later, in a beautiful passage about time, Augustine begs pardon for wanting to understand the passage of time by measuring it. He writes:

Is there one who will tell me that there are not three times—past, present, and future—as we learned as children and have taught children, but that only the present exists because the other two do not? Or do they also exist in that the future emerges from somewhere hidden as it becomes present, and again retires to somewhere hidden when from present it becomes past?

Time indicates permanence. It is not to say that we cannot become better. But every flaw within us, is also *of* us. Our poems track the progress of our humanity. They also hold dear our ugly flaws: the "somewhere hidden," which makes us human. The humanity we sheepishly run from, and ultimately, the humanity to which we retire.

At the Solstice, a Yellow Fragment

Our lord of literature
   visits my love,
they have gone below,
they have lost their way
among the tablets
of the dead—;

     preeeee—dark energy—woodrat
    in the pine, furred thing
        & the fine,
a suffering among syllables, stops
   winter drops from cold,   cold,
miracle night   (a fox
      deep in its hole under yellow
     thumbs of the chanterelles,
   (no: gold. Gold thumbs, Goldman Sachs
     pays no tax . . . (baby goats
in the pen, not blaming God,
    not blaming them—

(alias: buried egg of the shallow-helmet turtle
      [*Actinemys marmorata*]
alias: thanks for calling the White House
      comment line))))

For your life had stamina
from a childhood among priests
& far in the night,
beyond the human realm, a cry
released the density of nature—

THE STORY OF A POEM

For whom do you write? people sometimes ask poets. Even other poets ask this. My sense of an audience changes, sometimes in a single day! I write for myself, for the great dead, for a particular friend, for a living stranger, for readers after my time on Earth.

Who are you, reading this? Do I know you? Did you fall in love with poetry when you were young? Are you a rational person? A bird-watcher? A number-lover? A grower of kale? A hurt twin of the universe? Are you baffled by the bland reception of your first book? Are you a student assigned to read this essay? Do you like video games, Icelandic legends, field hockey? Does poetry offer relief from depression? Do you organize poetry readings at your local library? Did you set down a path for others? Did you set down your glass of wine? Are you that rare being, a satisfied poet?

. . .

This unique anthology proposes that poets might feel differently about their poems than the so-called world does. I sometimes read anthologies to see how contradictory energies are arranged like furniture in a hexagonal room. "Poetry makes nothing happen," wrote W.H. Auden famously and controversially (by which he did not mean poetry is not "relevant" but that there is a difference between what poetry can do and what political language can do). But poetry makes life happen by giving language and arrangement to the as-yet-unrealized anarchic experiences we bear, sometimes in great suffering.

•••

Some people say my poems are not easy. I don't believe poems are in themselves either easy or difficult; they take place in relationship to the knowledge we bring to them. Some of my favorite poems have interior hinges that are permanently loose and swing the gates around when someone passes by, poems that reinvent themselves when readers think about them in a new way.

As a young poet I didn't know one could create new models. In the '60s, the Internet didn't exist, of course; there was less leeway for poets to write beyond the dominant idioms. We imitated poets we admired, and that is certainly a good practice. But when I moved west, I found radical knowledge in the landscape and in literature to expand my own models and to make new arrangements. I realized that each poem could be a wild garden where myth, daily life, nature, and politics would coexist. Just as every body is a community and our guts are full of nonhuman entities, so every poem is a community.

•••

For this anthology I chose a poem from a book I wrote about western microseasons. The traditional four seasons have gotten plenty of attention in poetry. But the West Coast has dozens of microseasons and they are underrepresented. I drafted a poem every few weeks, inviting plants, animals, and the spirit world into each piece to include both science and magic.

The winter solstice, enchanting for its mystery, is a time of year I love. In our area there is little snow or ice. Fire danger is generally over; rains are underway, with nuthatches and cedar waxwings passing through. As solstice approaches, I feel an odd joy of an introvert from whom less is required. This joy has nothing to do with the commercialism of the holidays but is a mysterious force field. The light is shorter, softer, finer; our sea mammals are in winter migration; the journey into the self and into time can deepen. In our kitchen, spicy things are being prepared. I'm comforted by the thought of animals burrowing underground to be warm and hidden. The seasons exist in time and eternity.

...

Four more thoughts:

—The lord of literature: This came from my trance practice, a vivid mythic figure not based on any actual person but on an archetype of a companionable male figure. I've often been helped by such figures. Like many teachers, my husband and I can feel burdened at this time of the year. The lord of literature is invoked as a guide into a cave where dreams and the symbolic world can be summoned, even the "tablets of the dead" (great myths) to keep us connected to the eternal.

—Collage technique: Like many poets, I enjoy collage because it allows me to represent how the brain really works (not smoothly!). Proportions are established according to intuition and music. Sounds of winter birds, towhees and juncos, political references (Goldman Sachs, the multinational investment bank), the soul's processes, and chanterelles, those golden mushrooms that hide and nobly emerge in the short secret light, are here together. I often push my juxtapositions to the edge of sense while keeping emotion that will allow the heart to engage.

—Sentence fragments: Thoughts can be completed or not. There are half-statements about pond turtles and the voices in the White House comment line. This is a bit polyphonic. When friends say, *I'm trying to find my voice,* I always think, doesn't a poetic voice float among other voices? Some poems are like the lint trap in a dryer, snagging threads from the air.

—The end: an assurance to my poet-self and to the lover in the poem. Interior journeys in poems can be frightening, but poems can offer qualified wisdom, not necessarily absolute wisdom: "For your life had stamina / from a childhood among priests / & far in the night, / beyond the human realm, a cry / released the density of nature—" I believe this is true. Our lives have stamina, and we can have different kinds of priests. A cry in the night releases the obscurity of the natural world to make music and meaning, enigma and substance.

...

Poems offer opportunities to heighten odd, intense moments of experience, perception, and thought. We hope the poems we write in our present time might have value for longer than a single life span. If humans survive environmental peril, poetry can take us into the future and yet connect us with the particulars of our time.

Blood of my blood (walk away)

My father,
where would we be now
if you had just walked away
those times your fists grew tight
and your father's blood screamed
inside your skull for the crash
of knuckle against my mother's skull?

Where would we be
if you had turned your back
to whatever hot words boiled
from my mother's mouth,
from whatever insult you heard
or saw in whatever slight
or terrible gesture?

I'm left with a legacy of stitches
burned across her scalp,
of deadly household silence,
its ocean of unsaid seething . . .

I know the way I've prayed
that my hands would never
swing the weight of our fists
across my lover's face.

My father,
I'd wish you the patience
of both hands at your side,
of arms folded in front of you.

I'd wish you

the counting to 10
or 20
or 100,
I'd wish you both hands up
in surrender,
or behind your head
or behind your back
or buried in your pockets
or blocking her fists or slaps
as you back away

I'd wish you a swift retreat
when you felt your father's fist
rising against my mother's anger,
I'd wish you a clear path to the door
when you felt the world's whip
on your back in her tongue
in the heat of your marriage.

I'd wish you a walk around the block,
a fast car to squeal through streetlights,
a long bus ride into the afternoon,
a taxi waiting at the curbside,
a bike to ride furious into night,
or just the slam of a door behind you
instead of the slam of your fists to flesh.

I'd wish you one friend to call,
or two or twenty

begging you to stand down,
to remember what a man can lose
with the stroke of one blow:
love, respect, wife, children, family,
career, freedom, freedom
from the label *woman beater,*

I'd wish you the words to say
I'm leaving now before I lose it.
I'd wish you the knowing
when you were about to lose it.
I'd wish you shelter to find yourself,
before coming back home without rage.

My father,
I'd wish almost anything else in the world
than me, standing over you years later,
feeling my father's blood
surging in my fist.

But here we are, blood of my blood,
and the only gift I can give you
is that I've run from your blood in my blood
when my anger rose. I've tried to kill
the parts of you that took me so close
to killing.

My father,
where would we be now
if you had just walked away—

what if I weren't scrambling
through the years
through the rubble
to stitch together the shreds
of what I wish I'd been able to tell you—

I love you.

Now,

      I'm walking away.

———

This poem was inspired by the lack of a public service announcement for men. One that replaces the stereotype of men as bestial, predatory, and inclined to violence, with the understanding that men have the ability to make a choice in the heat of a moment. A PSA where a man is on the verge of losing his temper, when he may be feeling pressured beyond his ability to cope, when he may be experiencing actual physical violence initiated by a woman—and is about to lose control of himself and strike back. This poem is meant to trigger, to awaken the moment when a man might say to himself: "I need to leave this situation, this room, this house *immediately* before I lose control of myself."

    This poem is an effort to open a more extensive dialogue on intimate partner violence, acknowledging that in many instances such violence is bilateral and in as much as 40 percent of cases is initiated by women* . . . *blocking her fists or slaps / as you back away.* It is this poet's belief that unless this reality is engaged on some level, remedies to intimate partner violence will ever be shortsighted and hindered in their ability to end family violence. The poet also knows that there are many who will dispute the statistical evidence that bilateral intimate partner violence is an issue worth addressing. But the poet also knows

---

* See Murray A. Straus, "Women's Violence toward Men Is a Serious Social Problem" in *Current Controversies on Family Violence,* second edition, edited by Donileen R. Loseke, Richard J. Gelles, and Mary M. Cavanaugh (Sage, 2005).

    For more recent information concerning intimate partner violence, please see Emiko Petrosky et al., "Racial and Ethnic Differences in Homicides of Adult Women and the Role of Intimate Partner Violence—United States, 2003–2014" in *Morbidity and Mortality Weekly Report* (CDC, 2017), https://www.cdc.gov/mmwr/volumes/66/wr /mm6628a1.htm.

that there are men in the audience who have, without initiating violence, been slapped, kicked, shoved, thrown at, stabbed, scalded, burned, pummeled, spat on, and punched under extremely difficult circumstances and who have struggled to keep their composure, and thought that maybe they are weak for doing so. This poem is for them, and a call for them to recognize that they do the right thing by walking away from violence and violent relationships, and that they should continue to do so.

While writing the poem, I felt a need to be plaintive with the message, but I also had to frame it within my own understanding of the subject. Thus, the memories of my father's violence, and an attempt to reconcile with him, and at the same time a need for distance from the legacy of his destructive temper.

The poem begins with an earnest question, and then eventually employs the anaphora and plaintive nature of a list poem. The wishes pile up around me and my father, stacking up hopefully not just around us but also around the reader's comprehension that he does not have to resort to violence. The cascade of wishes is a wish for the reader to understand that he does not have to reciprocate violence with violence, that he has the option to leave the premises and spare himself and those closest to him the battering of his loss of control. Anaphora is, after all, something like a chant. And a chant is, after all, a common device in prayer. And a prayer is, after all, something as ephemeral as the moment one makes a decision for peace instead of violence.

Perhaps the most self-indulgent moment of the poem is the call for the reader to think of their own self-interest in the heat of the moment:

> remember what a man can lose
> with the stroke of one blow:
> love, respect, wife, children, family,
> career, freedom, freedom
> from the label *woman beater*

This poet made the judgment that the greater evil would be the commission of violence and not the avoidance of violence through self-interested self-discipline.

The poet hopes the poem was successful, because it was honestly the best he could do at the time, and he has come back to it over and over and finally threw up his hands and said, "That's the best I can do right now." The poet goes off to read the poem to his father.

Marina Tsvetaeva

In each line's strange syllable: she awakes
as a gull, torn
between heaven and earth.

I accept her, stand with her face to face.
—in this dream: she wears her dress
like a sail, runs behind me, stopping

when I stop. She laughs
as a child speaking to herself:
"soul = pain + everything else."

I bend clumsily at the knees
and I quarrel no more,
all I want is a human window

in a house whose roof is my life.

MY FIRST TSVETAEVA

It is August 19, 1991, and Gorbachev is imprisoned in Crimea and tanks
again roll into Moscow: I am fourteen years old.

Now, thirty years later, recalling that time, I see not the TV images
of a defiant Yeltsin on the top of the tank, his officially glorified, drunk
protest.

Instead, thinking of the August 19, 1991, Communist takeover, I see my mother's frightened phone calls from Odessa to her relatives in Moscow, and the lines not working. She is calling again. And the lines don't work.

I am a deaf boy who can't hear but sees his parents' fear. Middle of the night. Relatives call. On my mother's lips: strange news of the hundreds of sandwiches my mother's aunt makes, she is taking them to frightened boys in uniforms, in tanks, sent to take over the city.

My mother's aunt is hugging them, those boys who were sent to shoot her and others in the crowd. She is pouring them tea from her thermos. She is saying: I am your mother's age, don't shoot me.

1991 Communist takeover: my mother and father, five thousand miles from Moscow, in our tiny Odessa room, click the channels on TV. Father's hand twitches. On every TV channel: *Swan Lake* ballet. Mother's dry laugh: there are tanks in Moscow and all we see is swirling ballerinas.

August 1991: in Odessa there are no protests. Stepping into the tram I see a different quality to the silence as the tram shakes through streets: a crowd of people huddled inside watching one another. In a crowded silence, I notice how history takes up residence in our bodies.

‹Silence.›

Out of nowhere, in the middle of the moving tram, an old frail man stands up, shaking, and recites—shouts out, really—a poem by Tsvetaeva on the Nazi takeover of Czechoslovakia.

His body keeps shaking.

The tram stops. It isn't our stop; but the driver hits the breaks.

We are all quiet: the fragile man, holding himself up by placing his two hands on the shoulders of those around him, shouts the poem.

‹No one says a word.›

We watch history move inside bodies of others sitting and standing next to us.

It is as if he is reciting not to us but to the sidewalks, to the rooftops of this city, as the tram stills.

They took—hastily and took—openly:
Took mountains and their entrails,
They took coal and took steel,
From us lead they took—and crystal [...]

They took the sugar, and took the clover,
They took the West and took the North,
They took beehive, and took the haystack,
They took South from us, and the East. [...]

Took our fingers—and took comrades
But while we have spittle
in our mouths: The whole country is—armed!

These are lines of Tsvetaeva's poetry I have seen before on my father's lips:

"no pokuda vo rty sluna: vsya strana vooruzhena"

‹The tram is motionless for a few minutes.›
Then, it moves again.

What does history look like? I have no answer. All I see is this first public poetry reading of my life. It happens on August 19, 1991.

Brood

My chest is earth

I meant to write *my chest is warm*
but *earth* will do
                              to exhume a heart

  Beat

I meant to write
breathe

            Did you know I was alive the whole time

I was alive in the ground but torpor

        But torpor

Slowed beat

My chest filled like a jar with dirt

I mean
  dearth

For slow months at rest in the hole
I'd made in myself
      A frozen ground
   A ground in thaw

I mean
      Spring is coming
I mean
       I push the wet dirt with my mandible
I mean *jaw*

 Jaw

    Y'all

I know I am not a nymph in exhumation

 but would you please explain
      this half-remembered light

Exhumation, or What the Cicada Knows

"Brood" emerges not after being interred in the earth for seventeen years in a larval stage but after trying to text my new beloved in the early days of our relationship. The series of frustrating but evocative autocorrect suggestions—*earth* for *warm*?—belie the strangeness of what I was trying to write in the first place: a series of observations about my own body, awakening out of some slow time, some time of low feeling. It was winter, of course, as it mostly is in Western New York, and the bright light of my beloved's attention warmed me, pulled me out of my interment. And still, who would think to text, *my chest is warm*? Wrestling with the autocorrect highlighted how weird I was being by offering even stranger descriptions, descriptions that served as a kind of invitation. The poem accepts the invitation of the autocorrect with earnestness and curiosity. What would it mean if one's chest was earth, was dirt? What would it mean to follow the trail of that image, to go into the earth and emerge, to rise alongside an animal so patient at waiting, a guide that knows how to surface through the soil?

At the heart of my poetic practice is curiosity and a belief that I can learn how to be better at being a person by turning to nonhuman animals. The summer of 2011 in Nashville, Tennessee, brought the cicada into my life. Brood XIX emerged from the yard. The nymphs crawled onto my fence, their juvenile exoskeletons split open at the back. The new adults leaned back, near perpendicular, soft, white, and opaque, until they hardened into screaming jewels. What more could a poet ask for, right there on her own little deck? Yet I wasn't interested in the cicada only as fodder for metaphor. I wondered what I could learn from their life cycles. What I described earlier as patience is simply how the cicada lives. There is no option for a cicada's life that does not include time in the earth. Might it also be true, then, that there is no option for me but what happens? Might periods of long waiting be also integral to my life?

At one point, the speaker collapses into the cicada, via the transmogrifying magic of metaphor, but she stops, remembers what she is not, and pops out of the image. This is one of my favorite moments in the poem, the moment when the speaker, who had developed a mandible capable of biting through dirt, remembers she has a *jaw*. She remembers she is not a cicada, that the cicada is not human, that across difference there can be connection without assimilation.

Is this my best poem? Who knows! But I do know that I love this poem as an artifact of a time, as a record of thinking and coming into feeling. When I read it now, I am struck most by the playfulness that marks the movement of the poem. This playfulness reflects a strategy that I have come to rely on for most of my adult life: using play, with sound and language, to cut a pathway through feeling.

Yusef Komunyakaa

Crack

You're more jive than Pigmeat
        & Dolemite, caught by a high note
   stolen from an invisible saxophone.

I've seen your sequined nights
        pushed to the ragged end
   of a drainpipe, swollen fat

with losses bitter as wormwood,
        dropped tongues of magnolia
   speaking a dead language.

You're an eyeload, heir
        to cotton fields & the North
   Star balancing on a needle.

Where's the loot, at Scarlett O'Hara's
        or buying guns for the Aryan Nation?
   The last time I saw you, fabulous

merchant of chaos, you were beating days
        into your image as South African
   diamonds sparkled in your teeth.

Cain's daughter waits with two minks
        in a tussle at her throat,
   fastened with a gold catch.

You pull her closer, grinning up
        at barred windows, slinky
   as a cheetah on a leash.

You're the Don of Detroit,
        gazing down from your condo
   at the night arranged into a spasm

band, & groupies try to steady hands
        under an incantation of lights,
   nailed to a dollarsign & blonde wig.

Desire has eaten them from the
        inside: the guts gone, oaths
   lost to a dictum of dust

in a worm's dynasty. Hooded
        horsemen ride out of a Jungian
   dream, & know you by your mask.

I see ghosts of our ancestors
        clubbing you to the ground.
   Didn't you know you'd be gone,

condemned to run down a John
        Coltrane riff years from Hamlet,
   shaken out like a white sleeve?

Bullbats sew up the evening
        sky, but there's no one left
   to love you back to earth.

The speaker in "Crack" uses the language of urban insinuation as a choice of weapons to begin the search for a hurting truth. Indeed, innuendo delivers us into and through a music I hope unearths an answer. And such is the case with a novel I don't even remember the title of, but I can feel the idea of an evil that continues to haunt me, still residing in my psyche for years. A character called the Don of Detroit and his cohort discuss a code of ethics that demands they not push hard drugs into their community, or on their fellow citizens. But then the Don says, "We are going to push the hard stuff on the animals." This sounds like a war pledge. Of course, he is talking about Black and Brown people.

The title "Crack" sounds like a whip, without the false urgency of an exclamation point. In fact, "Crack" also sounds like the damage it does to families; especially, if we think about what it has done to Black families and communities throughout the United States. It is especially troubling when we attempt to confront this dilemma, this social phenomenon that took root shortly after the Civil Rights Movement during the 1960s and 1970s. And it is difficult for one not to think about what occurred after the Civil War, how much of the country organized efforts to roll back any progress for former slaves—after the undermining of Reconstruction sprang an onslaught of Jim Crow laws and ordinances.

And if we keep our eyes half open today, we cannot deny drugs have undermined whole communities. There are no two ways about this reality. How can we dig down to the quick of the matter? It is important to keep the galley of questions alive; no, I don't believe our government was involved, but there are those who think so. Could this have been possible? Was "crack" truly pushed into Black and Brown communities by white supremacists? Yes, they have the airplanes and yachts. Should we just back away from such questions, with our hands over our eyes, like wounded souls always searching for love? Well, for a moment, I wanted to cut the strings on the "Crack" poem, but then

I had to say no. Yes, perhaps there's something pulsing there in the blood sac, in the ugly idea. Could this be true? And I continue to say, Would someone please prove me wrong?

I remember how difficult it was to first trust each other in 'Nam. Could we look each other in the eyes, especially when the daily bad news from back home always seemed to find us even in tall thick elephant grass or at the hole-door of a tunnel. Yes, Hanoi Hannah seemed to have known the score.

Finally, after months of yes and no, I wrote the first three lines. And from the very beginning, the language of "Crack" was satirical. Just the mere mention of Pigmeat and Dolemite is a step toward the dozens—a page torn out of classical putdown artists. Both comedians were notorious during the so-called Chitlin' Circuit: both cut party records and appeared live, delivering character assassinations in roadhouses. Of course, Langston Hughes had mastered a slightly more literary insinuation and verbal folly with *The Best of Simple.*

Could an aspect of organized crime have been perfected through racial hatred? Was "crack" pushed into Black communities because of the minor advancement of a few Black folk? I have been troubled by evil within this "Crack" scenario; or, maybe simply I do not wish to believe Americans could be so methodically destructive to their fellow citizens. Yet, if we take a step back into time, we see inhumane evidence. Just gaze a moment into the eyes of faces captured in public hangings on postcards mailed across America (I doubt if such were airmailed overseas). Think about the selling of illegal moonshine doctored with Red Devil Lye mixed in #3 galvanized washtubs sealed with seams of lead.

Of course, those who would have been involved in such a deceitful enterprise wouldn't have necessarily been of the criminally elite with organized firepower behind them. The "Crack" poem may possess a hint of music of casting a spell or hex, but not a curse. Perhaps the speaker's voice is a trickster with a cache of information displayed for the reader or listener as an active participant, and the interaction often is prompted by a provocative question. A searching question such as this: "What was David Duke doing in Russia, teaching a seminar on Paul Robeson?"

Sometimes one may marvel at how easily evils can hold hands. And it seems such is the case with some of the crack dealers and rap industry, whose motto seemed *Anything to Bring the House Down.* Yes, the Civil Rights Movement had achieved a moral currency worldwide. But, of course, Dr. Martin Luther King, Malcolm X, and Fred Hampton had already been taken out—assassinated. Yes, sometimes deeds hook up like stanzas in a poem.

How does all this connect to the crack epidemic in Black and Brown neighborhoods across the USA? Yes, perhaps Americans have not only perfected elements of psychological warfare but also dealt in certain aspects of biological warfare on fellow citizens. The poem "Crack" is merely a nudge—not a philosophy. If anything, it is only a serious question. But I still don't know who has the answer. Maybe there's a good-hearted snitch out there, still moved by that moment when President Obama led the choir in a humanizing rendition of "Amazing Grace" at the Mother Emanuel Church in South Carolina. If so, please step forth, Brother or Sister.

Dorianne Laux

Arizona

The last time I saw my mother
she was sitting on the back patio
in her nightgown, a robe
thrown over her shoulders, the elbows
gone sheer from wear.

It was three months before her death.
She was hunched above one of the last
crossword puzzles she would ever
solve, her brow furrowed
over a seven-letter word for tooth.

I was staying at a cheap hotel, the kind
where everyone stands outside
their front door to smoke, a cup
of hotel coffee balanced
on the butt end of the air conditioner
blasting its cold fumes over
the unmade bed. The outdoor
speakers played *Take It Easy*
on a loop, and *By the Time*
I Get to Phoenix, and *Get Back.*

It wasn't the best visit. My sister's house
was filled with dogs, half-grown kids
and piles of dirty clothes. No food

in the fridge so we went out
and got tacos, enchiladas and burritos
from the Filibertos a few blocks away,
a squat tub of guacamole and chips,
tumblers of horchata, orange Fanta
and Mr. Pibb, a thousand napkins.
Everyone was happy while they chewed.

The state of Arizona is a box of heat
wedged between Las Vegas and Albuquerque.
Not a good place to be poor or get sick or die.
My mother rode on a train from Maine in 1953
—she was just a girl, me bundled in her arms—
all the way to California. I've tried to imagine it.

If you continue west on Route 66
it will branch upward and dump you
into the spangle of Santa Monica
where I used to live, and then you can
drive Highway One almost all the way up
the Redwood Coast to Mendocino.
I used to do that. I probably spent more time
in my car than in any house I lived in.

My mother never knew where I was.
She'd call and leave a message,
"This is your mother" (as if I might not
recognize her voice), "and I'm just wondering
where you are in these United States."
She used to make me laugh. The whole family
was funny as hell, once. Dinnertime was like
a green room full of stand-up comics.
That day, sitting with them over spilled salsa,
I saw the damage booze and meth can do
to a row of faces. The jokes were tired

and the windows behind them filled
with hot white sky, plain as day.

When I got back to the hotel it was getting dark,
but it had cooled off so I took a walk around
the parking lot. Strangers leaned out over
their second-floor balconies and shouted down
at their friends traipsing away in thin
hotel towels toward the tepid blue pool.
The moon was up, struggling to unsnag itself
from the thorny crowns of the honey locusts,
the stunted curbside pines.

I left my tall mother on the couch where
she was sleeping, flat on her back, her robe
now a blanket, her rainbow-striped socks
sticking out like the bad witch beneath
the house in the *Wizard of Oz*. But she
was not a bad witch, nor was she Glinda,
that was my mother's brother's wife's name.
We called her the bad witch behind her back.

My mother still wore her wedding ring,
even after she remarried. Why spend good money
on a new one when she liked this one perfectly well.
She always touched it like a talisman,
fretted it around her bony finger.
Three kinds of braided gold: white, rose and yellow.
By the end, the only thing keeping it
from slipping off was her arthritic knuckle.
I don't know what my sister did with it
after she died. I wonder if all that gold
was melted down in a crucible, the colors
mixing, a muddy nugget.

I do know that Route 66, in addition
to being called the Will Rogers Highway
and The Main Street of America,
was also known as the The Mother Road,
from John Steinbeck's *The Grapes of Wrath.*
My mother looked like a woman Walker Evans
might have photographed, with her dark
wavy hair, wide forehead and high cheekbones,
one veined hand clutching her sweater at the collar,
her face a map of every place she'd been,
every floor she scrubbed, every book she'd read,
every ungrateful child she birthed that lived or died,
every hungry upturned mouth she fed,
every beer she drank, every unslept night,
every cigarette, every song gone out of her,
every failure. Severe, you might say.
She always looked slightly haughty,
glamorous and famished.

I saw all the cars parked in that lot and wanted
to hotwire one with a good radio, drive away,
keep driving until the ocean stopped me,
then hairpin up the coast and arrive
like an orphan at Canada's front door.

If I'd known I'd never see my mother again
I wouldn't have done much different.
I might have woken her, taken her tarnished
shoulders in my arms, rocked her like a child.
As it was, I bent over her and kissed her
on the temple, a curl of her hair caught
for a moment in the corner of my lips.
This is my mother I thought, her brain
sleeping beneath her skull, her heart

sluggish but still beating, her body
my first house, the dark horse I rode in on.

———

I usually compose a poem long after the occasion of the poem. I need
time to process the event and see the larger world around me rather
than be confined to the tunnel vision of the occurrence. I need to
understand the aftermath and consequence to see/hear/feel if it reso-
nates, like a ringing bell or piano note that goes on beyond its ending.

And then my mother died, and I did not think, as Stephen Dunn
says in his poem "The Routine Things around the House":

> When Mother died
> I thought: now I'll have a death poem.

I'm not sure what I did think, but it might have been something like,
I'll never be able to write about her death. Or, *If I do, it won't be for years.*

But then, I couldn't sleep. I couldn't stop thinking about her and see-
ing her, hearing her voice, feeling her hands in my hands, smelling her
hair, tasting her perfume after she sprayed it into the air around her
then walked through the mist. And so I wrote, night after night, poem
after poem. I could not stop writing about her. Even when I wrote
poems about other things, I could not *not* write about her, always rid-
ing beneath or just above or throbbing in the center of every poem.
She was such a vast part of my existence on this earth, every particle of
her was inside me.

I wrote hundreds of these poems, though only twenty of them
would be chosen for my New and Selected: *Only as the Day Is Long.*
My mom had always been my muse, my mystery, my mother, and so
I have written about her from my first book on, what she was besides
being a mother: a nurse, one of the first paramedics, a pianist, a singer,
an avid reader, an intellectual, a political thinker, a crossword puzzle
in-ink solver, a fine dancer, a Katharine Hepburn–esque beauty, tall
and stately, raven-haired, a French woman with a touch of Micmac

Indian that stood out in her cheekbones. She towered above the men and women that surrounded her in the drab middle-class neighborhoods we lived in. It was difficult to see her as ordinary, though these are mostly the people I love and write about.

But she actually was ordinary. She was like every woman who had packed her bags to leave one edge of the country for another, to strike out on her own with a child in her arms, me, and see what was out there. She made an epic journey, and I didn't fully realize it until I wrote the poem that would be the penultimate and yet central poem of the book, "Arizona."

I didn't want anything from the poem except to write it, to see her again, in her element which was the family, as fully and truthfully as I could. I wrote it in one sitting, as an exercise in one of our weekly writing groups: ten words, a phrase, maybe a time of year or color, I can't remember now. But I used them all and it came out whole. I sent it to a friend who said it might need a bit of pruning but she liked it. I looked at it and saw what she meant, edited a line here and there, but otherwise chose to leave it as it was, messy, unrefined, raw.

The poem came in small chunks of memory. My mother as I remembered her most, in her nightgown and robe, bent over a crossword puzzle. Then I chose a memory of our last visit, to my sister's in Arizona, the hotel, the music. My sister's house, what we ate. Then the state of Arizona and what I knew of it, which led to Maine where my mother and I were born, then California where we settled. This led me down the roads I've traveled much in my life, Route 66, Highway 1. I heard my mother's voice again, calling me back, which led me to my family, the tables we sat around together over the years, then I found myself wanting to leave again, back to the hotel, but she wouldn't let me go. There she was, on the couch asleep, me gazing at her wedding ring, a thing I both loved and hated, both beautiful and a symbol of the man she married who had hurt us all. But I couldn't stay there, the road was calling me as it always had, and I suddenly saw how it was always a road that led me away from her and toward her at the same time, everything I both loved and feared was on that road, *The Mother Road*, something I had once researched on the Internet now usable. I gave into her then, my mother, in her silence, in her sleep, knowing now that she would be forever asleep, as I had slept in what seemed like forever in her arms. She was in my brain, my heart, my body. And then suddenly a poem by Matthew Olzmann I had recently read popped into my mind, "Letter to the Horse You Rode in on," and that became the last line of the poem.

It's an old phrase from the west when we all rode horses as our primary means of transportation. It was used as an insult, where instead of just insulting you, they insult your whole life. I don't imagine I've ever used the term but I knew it and knew what it meant. I'd hurled plenty of insults at my mother over the years, especially as a teenager, but now, after writing the poem and feeling her loss, after seeing her journey and knowing something of the pain of motherhood myself—the mistakes, the misfortunes, the muddled mystifying confusion of it—I saw her as a human being, a woman, who had done what she could to make a life, for herself, for me, for my brothers and sisters, and my heart was both sad and full.

As I say, I didn't want anything from the poem, and yet it took me on a journey that made me see not just my mother but also all mothers, how quietly heroic they are as they work. There are so many stories and poems about the heroics of men, the epic journeys they take, but so many fewer of women. And when I was done I felt I had raised my mother up to stand with the heroes of all time, and take her place among them, this ordinary woman who was extraordinary, who could now live on in the pages of a book. She was now my hero, my steed, the dark horse, which is usually a horse no one would bet on, but in this case a black horse, a spirit animal who symbolizes strength and passion and will carry you through difficult times, a horse no one should bet against.

Working Methods

LISTENING

I was falling asleep, wondering how to describe the poet's studio, when a voice said, "You have to be your own absence, with fifty percent deity."

woke up with: *I false—into arrangement; am out of it—deranged—*
woke up with: *hurry up is flamboyant and resolutional—*
woke up with: *as the ask progresses to a tiny new yes—*

My friend Dan says: Listen—Record—Orchestrate.

PLAYING

I was telling Dan that sometimes I get directions or lines for a poem by doodling—like how *"Isolato with a crown . . . / Isolato with a barge"* came from writing the word ISOLATO and putting a box around it and doodling around the box until one edge of it elongated into a tall thing wearing a crown-looking thing and the whole box looked like that thing on a barge.

He wanted to try it, so I said, "Give me a word." And he said, "Jang Kwon." And I said, "What's that?" And he said, "Heel-palm." And I knew it was a kung fu move—so I wrote JANG KWON and put a box around it and we each started doodling and writing commentary on each other's doodling and on each other's commentary and did some cutting and here is the poem:

JANG KWON (HEEL-PALM)

Like a tack, thunder defines the cloud.

Hand splaying, the fletching of an arrow

But the technique was not an arrow,
        hand or foot—

Was not an asking of what was next—:

The bent cherry
        shedding light above the flat and empty ground.

WATCHING

When the poem begins, a curtain draws back. There is a stage for the
mind's Moulin Rouge—

where the image gets its aria—

Pull the curtain: severed foot in a daisied green.
Pull the curtain: anatomical heart: a fortified city.
In the Panopticon, a throat in flames—

The eye swoops back, swoops in.

MAKING

Dream: *A test for my beginning poetry workshop: on a page is the barest
outline of a fish and the instructions say, "Now draw a more serious fish."*

Dream: *A poem hangs in the air like a curtain. It dismantles itself until all
that remains are single words. They shimmer: nouns and verbs.*

You must be your own absence, with fifty percent deity.
You must ask, Why this song, this seeing.

I don't remember writing this poem but I do recognize the signs that it's a pied beauty, orchestrated in my favorite mode: language cobbed from dream records, jotted hypnagogics, journal notes, scribbles on scrap paper that likely had an old poem draft, a page from a student paper from a long-gone semester, on the back.

I do remember it was a response to an assignment (circa 2003) from the *American Poetry Review* to describe my "studio"—which, in truth, at the time, was also my bedroom/living room/dining room/old converted horse stable with, I later discovered, no foundation under the brick floor.

Sitting in my one chair, a ratty thing from Pier One Imports (RIP), I noodled the assignment. How to describe, I thought, the poet's studio? Also, where was the cat getting those baby garter snakes it kept batting around, presenting on the bathmat as gifts?

(From the earth under the brick floor.)

I do remember scribbling, "Method, Method, what do you want of me?" the start of a famous quote by French Symbolist Jules Laforgue. It finishes: "You know very well that I have eaten the fruit of the Unconscious!"

• • •

The assignment of this anthology is: write about what poem of yours, poet, "matters most."

"Assignment" makes me think of teaching, and indeed this poem is an exegesis on, a set of instructions for, a series of examples of.

It is odd, mystic, teacherly, and emphatic. In this, it is a self-portrait.

• • •

I didn't choose this poem for the anthology; I read the anthology's assignment and this poem popped into my head.

Like a message from the earth under the brick floor—

For efficiency's sake and psychological relief, I make all kinds of decisions this way. It's preferable to agonizing over Choice, with its shadow companion Mistake.

And while I cannot attest to this poem's "bestness," I can attest to what makes it personal: the last couplet is a living *ars poetica* for me, a personal writing ethic.

...

Because "Working Methods" popped into my head in answer to this anthology's call, I have to ask: Why this song, this seeing?

Because, in its making, it surprised me? Shouldn't every poem you write offer you bits of revelation?

Because the methods it offers are implicit stays against self-protection? Stays against the voice of doubt and should, the voice egging you on to control and direct and be certain, so no one can tear the poem apart—but lively poems aren't creatures born from safety.

Because it was entirely delivered? Bits of language and thought and image calling out from diverse sources, their transformations just beginning—like baby snakes left on the bathmat by my familiar. I was able to rescue some from death—

Maybe this is why this poem said *Pick me!* for this anthology: to offer up a way to write, a way to think and live. What are poems for, anyway? To me, "personal best" arises out of the nexus of beauty, discovery, and aid.

I don't know any other way to traverse the crap paradise of this world than to treat everything that happens in it as an opportunity to learn something: *You must, You must,* you must be open and asking. Willingly unwilled. This is my mission and evangel.

This poem matters most because it is a guide.

Ada Limón

Adaptation

It was, for a time, a loud twittering flight
of psychedelic-colored canaries: a cloud
of startle and get-out in the ornamental
irons of the rib cage. Nights when the moon
was wide like the great eye of a universal
beast coming close for a kill, it was a cave
of bitten bones and snake skins, eggshell dust,
and charred scraps of a frozen-over flame.
All the things it has been: kitchen knife
and the ancient carp's frown, cavern of rust
and worms in the airless tire swing,
cactus barb, cut-down tree, dead cat
in the plastic crate. Still, how the great middle
ticker marched on, and from all its four chambers
to all its forgiveness, unlocked the sternum's
door, reversed and reshaped until it was a new
bright carnal species, more accustomed to grief,
and ecstatic at the sight of you.

———

I have always thought that "Adaptation" was a pivotal poem for me. I remember when I finished it, I thought something strange had happened. Something exciting to me, personally. I wanted to explore what it was to have a heart that changed. A heart that was changed by grief and would go on to change for love. But more than that, I think sonically and on an imagistic level it's a poem that's making many sporadic and eventful moves. It's driven out of instinct. It's a personal poem, yes, but it is full of my idiosyncratic music.

Ever since I was a child, I've been obsessed with Charles Darwin and the finches of the Galápagos Islands. Those eighteen species of finches with different sizes and, most significantly, different beak shapes that adapted due to different food sources. I wrote a report on them when I was in sixth grade for Ms. Steinberg's class for our science section. I remember thinking I'd like to only study birds and animals from then on. I loved the idea of adaptation, the idea of evolution, the idea of how we change.

When I started this poem some ten years ago, I thought, What if the heart was like one of the finches of the Galápagos? What if the heart changed its attributes based on what it was fed, or what food it could find? It made perfect sense to me. I even believe the poem started with the title. A rarity for me!

I started with the image of Darwin's finches in my mind of course, but then from the second line I loved the idea of my heart-birds being the "psychedelic-colored canaries." I also loved the sound of canaries instead of finches. I thought of the young heart, the starting-out heart, as something wild and excited at everything it sees. And then of course the next few lines lean into the retreat, the first hurts. The image of the great eye of a beast looking to harm the heart and how it becomes a cave full of the leftovers of life, the fire turned cold. I was particularly interested in what could freeze a fire, and how a frozen flame might look, like an ice sculpture made out of impossibly hard material. For me, these first two images immediately set up an interesting contrast. Then, on a craft level, the sounds and images felt heightened with an almost archaic drama.

Perhaps that's another thing I've always been interested in, in terms of this poem: the drama. I'm intrigued by the way this poem feels like its building toward something, the unknown of the "it" at the beginning. The setup of that mystery feels very dramatic, and though it could be seen as manipulative, for me it came naturally. I like a little drama.

The turn comes on the thirteenth line when the "it" is finally named as "the great middle ticker." That slow build to the realization always felt playful, the string that unravels when you pull it. Then, as we move toward the ending there's the phrase "from all its four chambers to all its forgiveness," and when that line came it felt like I had finished the poem.

But of course I hadn't. The heart needed to reach its final adaptation, or rather its most current adaptations. When the sternum is unlocked we get the idea of the cage again, and the canaries return to us. The word *carnal* mirrored *canaries* for me, which also added a sense of circular musicality. When the final two lines were written, I was so surprised by them. I hadn't realized that the core of the poem was that the heart would be more "accustomed to grief" and still be able to own that ecstasy of love.

This poem has always felt, forgive the cliché, close to my heart. On a craft level it's a frenzy of sonics and surreal imagery, but on a narrative level it is very much describing my own heart, the heart that was finally able to commit to a love and to accept a love. The poem came at an unexpected time, which is perhaps why it also feels significant to me. It wasn't just a casually written poem. It was a poem that was teaching me what I had been through, and showing me what I was ready for.

My First Husband Was My Last

If not for this one fond thought.
Trees wave their violent weight.
Heaved in air with storm's hand.
They confiscated my hair elastic.
They confiscate my bra, as each
could twist into a noose, my bra
wire sawed into a shiv. And we
were both stubborn. Asleep side
by side until the night before we
would never again sleep side by
side, neither of us was willing to
be put out, sleep on the couch.
Falling into bed, he dropped his
mouth by my ear to mutter deep
You'll drink yourself to death.

> Yet, we had much in common. We were both
> nocturnal as bats. We both smoked furiously.
> We each had a tendency to interrupt people
>
> mid-sentence though we each hated nothing
> more than being interrupted. We each had
> a tendency to hurl death threats. Enormously

seductive on first impression, once our targets
succumbed to our wiles, we stared back at their
love, appalled, our eyes dead diamonds.

We voted Democrat and loathed the rich.
We considered our intelligence unassailable.
We were unbearable. Yet my fondest memory

is when he arrived to bail me
out of jail and I do not intend
a metaphor. He was the only
one who saw me wince when
they tightened the handcuffs.
It was for his ear I'd quoted
Keats while being walked in
to the precinct: *Forlorn! The
very word is like a bell.* Never
an early riser, he did not fail
to arrive at the jail near-dawn.
I saw him pacing before that
Plexiglased partition serving
as portal to the room in which
I stood wearing the obligatory
orange jumpsuit in an orange
blaze thick with the company
of other women who had also
done some bad things wrong.

(I'd run a yellow light—he wanted his late-night
snack at the Country Kitchen—heard a siren stop
us, thought in fright my bowels might run loose
down the insides of my pant's leg, trying to walk
true to the line, so scared shitless was I, I suppose

any man who ever hopes to know me must know
this about me, that that's why I drove that night.)

Yet it's also true that night foretold how a shadow can strive
to overshadow another shadow (some of us, apparently, wake
only for these sorts of battles), for though I lay silent, assigned
to rest on the cell's concrete floor on a thin pallet, thrummed
to sleep by my cell mate's snores, the thought that I'd arrived
at a punishment so terrible made me feel a certain kind of pride.
Like my dear friend who died (who was not my ex-husband; *he*
is, I'm told, still very much alive), told me how he threw him-
self off from trees he'd climbed to see how he'd bleed when he
was a child, feeling the damp from concrete walls seep ache
into me became just another way I found to feel myself alive.

Yesterday I received notice
I'd failed to pay a civic fine,
a "penalty" I incurred from
an arrest that the court long
ago "dismissed." Although
I distinctly recall filling out
a sum of 200 bucks for that
particular money order back
in 1999, payable to the Iowa
Dept. of Motor Vehicles, no
record of this payment exists,
though judging by the clerk's
sharp glee tickling the ether
as she read aloud my crime
from off a computer screen,
although fourteen years have
slipped beneath us all, and I
can't remember that town's
street names, I'll never buck

the mean notoriety of that sad
local newspaper's entry: DUI.

I was placed in a 48 Hour Lock-Down Program as reprieve, as a first
time offender admitting my offense, a program operating, would you
believe, out the Heartland Hotel in Coralville: a bunch of drunks under
one roof being taught how to not use alcohol, reminded how each of us
had fucked up to the point each of us wept, among us a sixteen-year-old
who drove herself into a snowbank well over the legal limit, and me, I
was feverish to leave so as to be back with him, my first husband, who
had scored a good lead on pot from a friend I made over that weekend.

> Every bit of this is off-record. They confiscated
> my hair elastic. Even the mug shot, which I can
> only hope has been destroyed. Terrible-dark then,
> my hair rode its idiot storm atop my head. What's
> utterly queer yet remarkably clear in retrospect is
> how I felt a freak-urge to sneer or grin at the flash.
> They let me keep my underwear and socks. They
> confiscated my pocket change and wedding ring.

And if not for that one moment
when I stood within the gaggle
of orange-suited women (one of
whom growled, *Drunk driving?
You'll be back!*) that I saw him
pass before the Plexiglas as he
saw me, looked back, and he'd
mouth to me against it all, *You
look beautiful,* my stare drained
within the fluorescence, could I
forget any of it ever happened?

> *He told me I would die* as I lay
> beneath our shared coverlet. He

told a shared acquaintance I did
not care enough for the written
word. This was, in itself, blasphemy.
So I was the cunt who cut his vocal cords.
Or I was rich and hid my treasure.
He kept company with petty thieves.
His one friend stole coins out of laundry machines.
He's familiar to me as a dust mote.
He's familiar to me as the carved
wood masks we hung on our walls.
He's agape, always agape.

My first husband was my last.
He's my Love Canal.
It's a miracle anyone ever married me.
It's a miracle anyone ever married him.
He's digging himself up in Transylvania.
He's pulling the stake out of his heart with his yellow teeth.
His awful teeth aren't his fault.
He was raised inside a tin can.
He was suckled with corn syrup instead of breast milk.
I think of him at the polls.
I feel his thoughts collect like chalk dust in my nose.
I wake up in a sweat.
I wouldn't be surprised if I woke up next
to him tomorrow. We are celebrating
the Fourth of July. I have brought home
a rotisserie chicken, which we enjoy
pulling apart and licking its grease
from our fingers, and later we'll find
ourselves in our bed, the bed in which
we will make death threats to one another,
upon which we shall blame one another all
our bitter long-lives.

I once slammed the door in his face so hard
if he'd been standing an inch closer his fangs
would've been knocked down his throat. Or,

rather, landing ass-flat at his door's parting
slap, tailbone cracked, I chose to clatter back
down the hall, my pincers snapping through

the smoke-waters we'd made of our habitat.
The only reason we got married was because
we didn't know one another. But it is not true

that I chased him with a kitchen knife, ever.

On "My First Husband Was My Last"

I wrote the first draft of this poem in 2009. I felt cynical back then. It
seemed to me like all the poems I was reading in magazines resem-
bled the cars I drove beside on three-lane highways, identical makes
and models, and little variation between those. The nostalgic poem
eyeing family dysfunction through chiseled metaphor. The lubricated
poem shimmying alongside theory, making no real sense. Surrealism
so mass manufactured you might find it discounted at T.J. Maxx. The
extremely proficient ekphrastic. More than anything, I despised the
proficient ekphrastic.

I hated my poems, too, of course. I wanted to write something that
ran counter to them, something elegant.

But I have never been elegant.

I nursed the idea that my third book would be airy and erudite, a
sort of lofty series of elegies strung along the clouds, a semblance of
removed yet pained poems unlike anything I'd heretofore been able
to write. I wanted nothing to do with the heavy-handed, emotional

plunges my poems had always dragged me into: their lyrical spin cycles and insistence on the lurid. I deserved a vacation not only from the typical habitats my poems occupied but also their habits. I wished to write at a remove.

"My First Husband Was My Last" might not have broken through if I hadn't just had a baby. I was completely exhausted and had no use for conventions to which I'd previously cleaved. I didn't care if people might associate me with my speaker. When the title came to me, out of the blue, probably when I was attached to a breast pump, I laughed out loud. The poem announced itself as the voice of my next book, heralding poems that would move even further into the realm of the lurid. So much for elegant poems.

"My First Husband Was My Last" is about failure.

Formally, this poem took many years. I repositioned and rearranged the stanzas too many times to go into here. I was most worried about positioning the pin of this poem, which is the moment at which the speaker is done in. She sees her husband through the Plexiglas window as she is being held with other women in jail, after being arrested, and she is wearing the orange jumpsuit. The husband sees her, meets her eyes, and mouths that she is beautiful. This appeals to her vulnerability and vanity. She bites.

Being arrested for drunk driving when I was twenty-nine was something I did not speak or write about. Thinking about it made me sick with shame.

So I was taken by surprise by this poem's sudden appearance. It arrived whole. It was uncharacteristically long and unwieldy. I had no idea how to revise it. Also, it made light of situations that I'd long held in fragile regard. It laughed at me, and it made me laugh. The poem appalled and delighted me.

But the poem is also about how things will come back to haunt you. The writing of this poem occurred between 2009 and 2014. In 2013, I went to a DMV in New Jersey to get a new driver's license. I was prevented from doing so because I owed a fine to the State of Iowa that dated back to the time of my arrest in 1999. At the time, I had been told everything would be wiped from my record. And I had a distinct memory of preparing a money order for the amount of $200.00, the amount the woman I was now speaking to on the phone claimed I owed them. I could feel her reading my infraction from the computer screen in front of her. In her voice I sensed judgment.

I think this poem is nostalgic, too. I will never have a first husband again. There were a lot of things I liked about him. And he lives in my memory the way the smell of smoke never leaves a house that's had a fire.

On the B Side

The song ends because the beginning
doesn't jump-start again: red smudge

of a mouth, lipstick all over the place
like the afterthought a comet leaves

on its way out. What makes this moment
unfold like a woman raising herself

up from an unfamiliar couch? Honky-
tonk in the blue honey of an eyeball?

Perfume & its circus of heart-shaped
introductions? Innuendo always

stumbles in the lead-in, like a man
pawing around for his broken spectacles

after waking up in the world's stubble.
Hand over hand he paws, through

guitar picks & record changers, busted
gut strings & clothing strung with

familiar vibrato outside the window.
He could be Bowie himself, exhausted

by skyscrapers cracked in the aftermath
of a smile. His eyes aren't different

colors. They just have different focuses.
He could be a whole lot of nothing:

thinning hair, low change in his right
pocket jingling down the stairs.

He was given all of it & stole the best
of the rest. Even without glasses,

he sees her nearly dressed: 33⅓ rpm
staticky in the lead-out's harmony.

You're Not Alone

Poetry is language in balance. It is words arranged in unexpected patterns that can be translated or expanded upon in habitual yet surprising ways. Like the best jokes, poems situate us in the secrets of life before cracking open with surprise. Like the best declarations of belief, poems force us to reconsider our internal geographies because of whatever we've learned at the bus stop or in the garden. On a fundamental level, poems create symmetrical movements of sound and feeling—heartbeats of vowels and consonants—to frame the many textures of disbelief and delight around us.

There is so much more to poetry than these basic shapes—duende, scraped knees, sonnets, shattered loves, and lost trumpets—but the art operates based on knowable arrangements of feeling and music.

Simply put: all poetry is made up of different kinds of patterns. I became a poet in part because I'm fascinated by patterning, proportionality, and the irrefutable exquisiteness in balanced things. Saying I'm "fascinated" is really a jazz hands way of saying: I'm obsessed with matching in all parts of my life.

I've had a compulsion for matching for as long as I can remember, but I first recognized it while my family lived in Section 8 housing in Indianapolis in the 1980s. One of the many difficult things about being poor is that you often end up with incomplete, secondhand things—puzzles missing pieces, games with instructions but lacking the necessary parts, a four-place dinnerware set with only three plates, and even the remaining three are chipped or cracked.

This wasn't necessarily a bad thing. We were broke, but we usually had some food to put on those plates. I wasn't alone and had a sister and brother to help me piece together those almost-puzzles. But the incompleteness of everything around me led to a preoccupation with figuring out what was missing, and a desire to make things whole. I wanted—and still want—things to be unbroken, connected, and in balance. Ben Okri said that a poet "suffers our agonies as well and combines them with all the forgotten waves of childhood." For me, there seemed to be patterns inside the patterns in those waves, but I couldn't figure out their significance. What I did understand, though, was there needed to be some symmetry—of sound, of color, of shape—otherwise the other things around me would collapse in lonely and suffocating ways.

All of this is congruous with basic attraction in the world as well. Because of perceptual bias, symmetry is one of the most important indicators of beauty. That attraction applies to physical features, suit patterns, and guitar riffs in songs. It applies to lyric verse and sometimes to the world at large. Perfectly mirrored wing patterns can be found on the butterflies most people recognize as beautiful, but not on birds that may or may not be pleasing to the eye. The size and shape of bird wings are proportional, but the feather patterns can diverge so that their wings offer the impression of balance, but without true symmetry. The idea of beauty without its underlying satisfactions.

Their beauty isn't legible; it has to be worked for.

Legibility is an obstacle that exists in all art forms and especially in poetry, since so many of the structures inside of the poem are grounded in the poet's head. The best of us find ways to unpack the interior through music or image. For example, Robert Hayden's harmonious language in "Those Winter Sundays" where the patterns of sounds—the l's in "blueblack cold" and the d's in "cracked hands that ached"—are all framed by "the chronic angers" of the house the speaker describes. Or Lucille Clifton's "at last we killed the roaches," where the images of violence—"i swept the ceiling and they fell / dying onto our shoulders, in our hair / covering us with red"—weave a pattern of "O" whose sounds not only show destruction but also show us the place in which the poem exists and where the speaker is inside that world.

"On the B Side" is striving for a similar kind of musical symmetry. The patterns of sound present themselves openly inside the couplets, evoking the proportioned and lonely silence after a record ends. It's not clear from the title, but the poem was inspired by "Rock 'n' Roll Suicide," in which David Bowie's speaker reminds everyone listening that they are not, in fact, alone. What a vital reminder right now. There are other examples of patterning as well: the middle-aged guy in the middle of the poem who can't see without his glasses, fumbling around for some other definition of post-apocalypse beauty. There's a reference to Prufrock there, too, as the consummate midcareer whiner.

I hope that all these things line up in the end so that the poem becomes both a treatise of and the language for balanced lyricism. Precision, too: words in their best getups in the habit of an accidental *ars poetica*. It's comforting to me to find those moments of assonance or consonance inside the lines. The sounds are like the forgotten waves Okri spoke of, but transformed into echoes and patterns of my twenty-first-century trudge. For the brief expanse of the poem, everything gets to be matched and in balance, even as the world around the poem and around me continues to spin sideways.

Airea D. Matthews

Sexton Texts Tituba from a Bird Conservatory

for Margaret Walker and Molly Means

Fri, July 2, 7:07 PM
"Eat, the stones a poor man breaks,"

Fri, July 2, 7:18 PM
Still stale as they were
when Memaw died,
half-mad on working-class
hunger; plumpness thinned
to a chip of lamb's bone,
legs decayed, necrotic.

Fri, July 2, 7:26 PM
Running is a game
for the young. Women
of a certain age, root.

Fri, July 2, 9:09 PM
Some rot gashing cane
with dull machetes. Sinking in
clay around 10-foot stalks when
all the while they could have been
coal-eyed peacocks, lean deep-water
ghosts, spunforce bladefeathers,
fear itself.

Fri, July 2, 9:11 PM
Can you believe I still carry
the knife my husband gave me?
I gut, hollow, and scrape
soft spoil from cavities, but
what's dead is pretty well empty.

Fri, July 2, 9:21 PM
Good on you. Makes for easy work.
My people are steel-clad nomads
at the full-metal brink. None
know what's in the chamber,
staring down our barrels.

Fri, July 2, 9:32 PM
There's 2 ways to terrify men:
tell them what's coming,
don't tell them what's next . . .

Fri, July 2, 9:55 PM
(2/2) deathbed—herons,
black merlins, white-necked
ravens, mute cygnus, Impundulu—

Fri, July 2, 9:54 PM
(1/2) Pales lower as light approaches.
Memaw felt all kinds of birds
hovering near her

Fri, July 2, 10:07 PM
What did Impundulu want?

Fri, July 2, 10:10 PM
Wondered myself. She named
ancestors and gods I'd never
met—
limbs of Osiris in Brooks Brothers,
Isis in Frederick's of Hollywood,
Jesus in torn polyester.

Fri, July 2, 10:12 PM
Ah, the birds wanted them then.

Fri, July 2, 10:17 PM
No. She said: *They waitin'...*
for you.
Then she died,
eyes wide,
fixed on me

Fri, July 2, 10:28 PM
Dinn, dinn, dinn—
Dying's last words
mean nothing. What wants you
dead would have your head.

Fri, July 2, 10:29 PM
LOL! But I'm not dead, huh?

Fri, July 2, 11:21 PM
I'm not dead, right?

Sat, July 3, 3:00 AM
Anne? I'm not, right?

In Plato's dialogue *Theaetetus,* I find myself continually drawn to the question of knowledge and inspired by Euclid's declaration: "I may observe that I have introduced Socrates, not as narrating to me, but as actually conversing with the persons whom he mentioned. . . . I have omitted, for the sake of convenience, the interlocutory words 'I said,' 'I remarked,' which he used when he spoke of himself, and again, 'he agreed,' or 'disagreed,' in the answer, lest the repetition of them should be troublesome." As a writer, I return to both the efficiency of this omission and the invitation it offers. By vacating the diegetic markers emblematic of recounted stories— "I said," "she said,"—readers experience the story as it happens instead of reporting a dialogue as it's told. This narratological technique embodies interiority, persuades an intimacy between the speaker/s and the audience, and reduces the distance a narrator imposes.

I am often seeking ways to bridge distances between bodies and ideologies on the page and in real life, and I've come to believe that conversation is a powerful medium of understanding. "Sexton Texts Tituba from a Bird Conservatory," published in *Simulacra,* carries the same spirit. When I read the classics, I interrogate their forms and question whether contemporized versions of them exist. There are many examples of the dialogic, but the text message is compelling to me. Much like *Theaetetus,* text messaging reads like an archival transcript and lacks conventional diegetic markers. In text message poems, this absence creates an indeterminacy around speech and a crosstalk/parataxis that makes for pleasant confusion and encourages readers to produce their own meaning.

At the heart of my poem, readers find themselves thrust into a text conversation between the poet Anne Sexton, who committed suicide in 1974, and Tituba, a formerly enslaved West Indian woman among the first accused in the 1692 Salem witch trials. Both women lived in Massachusetts during completely different time periods and held different social standings and ethnicities. Here, we find these two women considering the undeniability of death; one with fear: "I'm not dead, right?" and one with resolve: "What wants you / dead would have your head." Their own differences and relationships to power, or lack thereof, surely informed their worldviews and positionality just as they did with Socrates and Theaetetus's musings. In the poem and the dialogues, it's remarkable that no conclusion is reached on either of their two respective subjects—death and knowledge.

The vacancy where an answer would be leaves room for nuance and uncertainty, and in that spaciousness, another view might emerge. As Tituba anxiously wonders about Impundulu, a bird in South African myth that is passed down from mother to daughter and ensures immortality, Sexton takes a more stoic view—"What wants you / dead would have your head." Between Tituba's and Sexton's positions on death, a tension emerges between Western and more indigenous

African beliefs. Do we reach the end at the end, or do we continue on? If Tituba held the faith of her ancestors, her spirit would go on. If Sexton held the beliefs of many Westerners, death is conclusive. Unlike Western texts where closure predominates, this poem poses a question as yet another nod to uncertainty and infinity. If the end of a poem is its own sort of death, I thought it best to leave the conceit open-ended. After all, some knowledge, like death itself, is best saved for a later time when the inevitable answer is revealed.

My Boy's Red Hat

At last I'm alone with my lover. Alone
As the music pours around the room
The proud trumpets the wheezing saxes
My hero is wearing his large red hat
And he is sad. The music is slowing.
I watch him strut to the full-length mirror
And his face wears the colors of all the fading
Flowers of his orchestra. "Music's Sorrow"
My friend this hero has worn his hat
Three times before. Once when dawn was breaking
Up his friends. Bright foam of sixteen year-olders
Full of lovely butterflies. Again,
When he scoured the west coast for their bodies
And he was their corpses in summation.
He hopes the music keeps playing. And he wears
His red hat now, same broad brim.
        Makes his torso seductive.
And he wears it at the Opera the
Ballet the festivals of unnamed rabbits crying
In the night. He wears it
In his small painting, "Charcoal Baby"
"Charcoal, baby." He utters to me.
Hands me his self-portrait and I cry.
It is invisible. He will never know.
Now he is crying on my lap. This is a mother's hat.
I am a fighting woman but what can I do

With my wounded son who floats through rooms
Like the one true phantom?
Warmly proud of his broad-brimmed hat.
His invisible naked stage. My boy.

November 8

THE OPPOSITE SEX

I was in an Alice Notley workshop at St. Mark's Church in Manhattan's
East Village. It was 1975 and I was twenty-five. Alice was the first poetry
workshop leader I had ever had who gave us assignments. I found
them demeaning. I felt like I already knew how to write a poem so an
assignment seemed designed for someone genuinely clueless, which
I wasn't. A few weeks into the class I had begun to be intrigued. I was
willing to give her the benefit of the doubt so we used a Red Grooms
piece, a blue drawing of Jean Harlow, one evening to generate a poem
in which someone was sitting on the porch in my big white sneakers
making jokes about nature. I liked what I got. It was an accident gener-
ated from somebody else's poet-mind, Alice's. I didn't know how that
happened (the poem), and the next week she asked us to write a pan-
toum, which remains one of my favorite received forms. I was forced
out of my comfort zone and landed in somewhere else to play. To be an
artist in. I began to realize I was playing Simon Says with Alice, a child-
hood game in which you would fulfill the requirements of the request
of the person playing Simon, but something else happened along the
way. In the game as kids we simply had fun (but fun was never simple)
and everyone had a different pace and the game kept going faster and
faster. In Alice's assignments, what became interesting was the mul-
titude of responses to "the same" assignment. Clearly, based on our
responses, we did not understand the assignment in the same way at
all. And the week she assigned the poem that I've submitted for this

anthology she clearly threw *me* a curve, if not anyone else in the room. She asked us to write a poem from the position of the opposite sex. The immediate response in my head has been one of the most telling moments in the history of my understanding of my own gender and maybe gender itself. And writing, too. I thought, *opposite* of what? I didn't mean I was sexless or nothing in some way. I just meant that my gender was entirely unstable. I didn't know what Alice wanted. Did she want me to write a poem from a position opposite from what people saw me as? How did people see me? Did I know? How did I see myself? Was it who I dreamed of being, who I fantasized about being when I read books or thought about my friends and the people I saw in the world? Who was I? What was I? There was no still place I could begin my imaginary portrait from. It forced me out of a safe position of appearances and into a true avant-garde of soul. What did I want? I wanted to be a beloved son. I wanted to be Jesus. I wanted to be the protected suffering god/human in the pietà. I wanted to be wounded in a war and taken care of by a woman. I wanted my mother to love me like she loved my brother. I might need to manufacture that condition for myself. I wanted to be hurt as only men are. I wanted to be a player in that dance. So I told that story the best I could at twenty-five. It's ponderous in a way I would never write now. But it's vulnerable probably in a way I'm no longer capable of, because though I hope to be always writing a different poem from the ones I've written before, I've never felt so raw in my becoming both a poet and an interesting female man, my own son somehow, and I write with him always and definitely with her and I think the act of writing is truly, deeply gendered and the window is open today still.

The Pacific Written Tradition

In 2010, I read aloud from my new book
to an English class at one of Guam's
public high schools. After the reading, I

notice a student crying. "What's wrong?"
I ask. She says, "I've never seen our culture
in a book before. I just thought we weren't

worthy of literature." I wonder how many
young islanders have dived into the depths
of a book, only to find bleached coral and

emptiness. We were taught that missionaries
were the first readers in the Pacific because
they could decipher the strange signs

of the Bible. We were taught that missionaries
were the first authors in the Pacific because
they possessed the authority of written words.

Today, studies show that islander students read
and write below grade level. "It's natural,"
experts claim. "Your ancestors were an illiterate,

oral people." Do not believe their claims.
Our ancestors deciphered signs in nature,
interpreted star formations and sun positions,

cloud and wind patterns, wave currents and
ocean efflorescence. That's why master navigator
Papa Mau once said: "If you can read the ocean

you will never be lost." Now let me tell you
about Pacific written traditions, how
our ancestors tattooed their skin with defiant

scripts of intricately inked genealogies,
how they carved epics into hard wood
with a sharpened point, their hands,

and the pressure and responsibility of
memory, how they stenciled petroglyphic
lyrics on cave walls with clay, fire,

and smoke. So the next time someone tells you
our people were illiterate, teach them
about our visual literacies, our ability

to read the intertextual sacredness
of all things. And always remember: *if we
can write the ocean we will never be silenced.*

━

I wrote this poem in 2015, and as soon as I finished revising it, I felt it
captured something essential about who I am as a poet and human
being. I am an indigenous Pacific Islander from Guåhan (Guam),
where I was born and raised. When I was fifteen years old, my fam-
ily migrated to California, where I would graduate from high school,

college, and graduate school. I was fortunate to attend the MFA program at the University of San Francisco, where I completed my first poetry manuscript, which focused on my native Chamoru culture and the history, politics, and environment of Guam. This manuscript would be published as my first book in 2008. Despite the fact that I had lived away from my homeland for thirteen years at that point, poetry was a vessel through which I could still feel connected and rooted.

In 2010, the Guam Humanities Council invited me to be part of a literature and politics initiative that they were organizing. This trip home would be the first time I returned in fifteen years. As part of the project, I visited public high schools throughout the island, the community college and university, and I conducted several public performances and talks. One of the most profound memories I have of that trip was when I met with a senior honors English class. After I performed my poetry, I noticed that a student was crying. When I asked whether she was feeling okay, she said: "I've never seen our culture in a book before. I just thought we weren't worthy of literature." She was referring to the long colonial history of Guam, which has been a territory of the United States since 1898. In school, children are taught American culture, history, and literature, and our own indigenous arts and identities are marginalized or, worse, completely erased. This moment stayed with me long after that trip because it reminded me about the power of literature, especially for people from colonized places.

I wrote this poem, "The Pacific Written Tradition," five years after that encounter. The poem begins by recounting the moment with the student, and then moves into a reflection about how our invisibility within the literature we are taught in school creates a harmful atmosphere for Pacific Islanders. I address other stereotypes in the poem as well, including the idea that native peoples come from "illiterate" and "oral" cultures, which is often used to explain why Pacific students read and write below grade level. The poem, then, becomes a space where I can subvert this damaging stereotype and insist on the dynamic and brilliant history of literacy within the Pacific. The poem ends on a note of empowerment, with a direct message to young Pacific Islanders.

I wanted to include this poem in *Personal Best* not only because it captures a moment that is personally meaningful to me; it articulates a Pacific-centered and indigenous conception of poetics, and it delivers a meaningful and inspiring message. I always perform this poem when reading in front of Pacific Islander audiences, and it always resonates, especially the last line. I am grateful for all this poem has taught me, and I am thankful that this poem will have new life and greater circulation through this anthology.

The Robots

When they choose to take material form they will resemble
Dragonflies, not machines. Their wings will shimmer.

Like the chorus of Greek drama they will speak
As many, but in the first person singular.

Their colors in the sky will canopy the surface of the earth.
In varying unison and diapason they will dance the forgotten.

Their judgment in its pure accuracy will resemble grace and in
Their circuits the one form of action will be understanding.

Their exquisite sensors will comprehend our very dust
And recreate the best and the worst of us, as though in art.

As Though

As I entered my teenage years, when my mother was bedridden after
a concussion, suffering from vertigo, headaches and painful sensitiv-
ity to light and sound, sometimes threatening to kill herself, she and I
shared a devotion to science fiction. We two read the same copies of
books and magazines but we did not discuss them beyond an occa-
sional "That one was good" or "It's pretty long."

I think the short, declarative sentences of my poem "The Robots" may reflect the pleasure I took in those days from the propulsive confidence of sheer *story*.

Many of the books (Asimov, Bradbury, Dick, Heinlein, van Vogt) and magazines (*Astounding, Galaxy, If*) came from the public library. We also bought a few, and somehow she had found a soldier stationed nearby at Fort Monmouth who shared our taste. We traded with him by the carton.

Studies of science fiction trace the many ways the genre has been a form of social criticism, from Philip K. Dick through Stanisław Lem, to Octavia Butler and beyond. For Sylvia Pinsky and me, maybe freedom to enter social arrangements unlike our daily reality compelled us as readers. Our family of five people lived in a two-bedroom, one-bath apartment on the shores of a white peninsula in a Black neighborhood. But for my mother and me the reading was a matter of appetite, not theory. We consumed what we read like meals or treats.

Cultures vary. Japanese presentations of robots usually portray them as benign and helpful, unlike most American and European works. Another cultural difference, not about robots as such, is in the chorus of Greek tragedy, where the male performers, moving in mechanical, metrical precision like military drill, chant in unison their lines that are in the first person singular. In actual battle, shoulder to shoulder, thrusting spears, by chanting they could make themselves into a human tank.

Benevolent circuitry; poetry recited in mechanical unison: ideas I resist but recognize, in those cultures unlike mine, modern Japan and ancient Athens. If poetry's imagination works toward freedom from clichés and expectations, those two visions of social identity, alien yet familiar, offer me some hope of leaping a few inches upward, to look around me from above my limited time and place.

When I first read the Greek tragedies, I learned that for Aristotle the highest form of action was *theoreia:* a movement of the soul toward understanding. Beholding.

My mother did not kill herself, and her symptoms over the years diminished, though they never ended. And who could forget them? My poem emphasizes the robots as creatures of memory. *Memory:*

routinely, a central term in robotics and artificial intelligence. It is also a perpetual emotional dilemma. For example: how should I, how can I, how might I remember my mother's distress and my dread of it?

We in my generation remember when floods, droughts, famines, plagues, earthquakes, and forest fires were called "natural" disasters. But the helpful machines we made and instructed to work for us create the disasters, as our agents. The calamities are mostly industrial, not natural. My mother's concussion came from a fall through fiberglass insulation where she thought there was a floor: misapplied or misunderstood architecture, in the boom year 1951.

In this poem, my ethereal robots in their flawless ritual have recorded and can reenact "the best and the worst of us." Possibly the most important two words in the poem are in the next phrase, "as though":

And recreate the best and the worst of us, as though in art.

An early experience of the harms and destructions of the irrational have allowed me to appreciate (and even idealize?) the rational, as in this poem's robots. But the art of poetry is a matter of *as though*: the intuitive, the suprarational, and—as a thing of pitches and rhythms and images—it emanates from the fleshly body and its actions. Our art is an action: it moves us mortals as it moves.

We clever animals have needed to imagine creatures better than ourselves. Even the petty, misbehaving Olympians, those liars and rapists, are perfect essences of their natures. Christian angels are creatures of pure reason, like the angelic Houyhnhnms of Jonathan Swift, who do not grieve. We grieve that our inventive craving for perfection may destroy life on Earth.

Constantly, every day of my life, I feel a dialogue between perfection and imperfection—in what I read, in what I write, in what I think and feel. In another of my poems that I considered for this book's assignment (there are no single "bests" of course), "Ode to Meaning," I speak to meaning in the second person:

After my mother fell on her head, she became
More than ever your sworn enemy. She spoke
Sometimes like a poet or critic of forty years later.
Or she spoke of the world as Thersites spoke of the heroes,
"I think they have swallowed one another. I
Would laugh at that miracle."

In my poem the perfect robots can only seem to make art, as though
they were us, their imperfect, needful makers—as though we know
what we are doing.

chronic

were lifted over the valley, its steepling dustdevils
the redwinged blackbirds convened
vibrant arc their swift, their dive against the filmy, the finite air

the profession of absence, of being absented, a lifting skyward
then gone
the moment of flight: another resignation from the sweep of earth

jackrabbit, swallowtail, harlequin duck: believe in this refuge
vivid tips of oleander
white and red perimeters where no perimeter should be

     here is another in my long list of asides:
why have I never had a clock that actually gained time?
that apparatus, which measures out the minutes, is our own image
        losing, forever losing

and so the delicate, unfixed condition of love, the treacherous body
the unsettling state of creation and how we have damaged—
isn't one a suitable lens through which to see another:
     filter the body, filter the mind, filter the resilient land

and by *resilient* I mean *which holds*
     which tolerates the inconstant lover, the pitiful treatment
the experiment, the untried & untrue, the last stab at wellness

choose your own adventure: drug failure or organ failure
cataclysmic climate change
or something akin to what's killing bees—colony collapse

more like us than we'd allow, this wondrous swatch of rough

why do I need to say the toads and moor and clouds—
in a spring of misunderstanding, I took the cricket's sound

and delight I took in the sex of every season, the tumble on moss
the loud company of musicians, the shy young bookseller
anonymous voices that beckoned to ramble
        to be picked from the crepuscule at the forest's edge

until the nocturnal animals crept forth
        their eyes like the lamps in store windows
                forgotten, vaguely firing a desire for home

hence, the body's burden, its resolute campaign: trudge on

and if the war does not shake us from our quietude, nothing will

I carry the same baffled heart I have always carried
        a bit more battered than before, a bit less joy
for I see the difficult charge of living in this declining sphere

by the open air, I swore out my list of pleasures:
sprig of lilac, scent of pine
the sparrows bathing in the drainage ditch, their song

the lusty thoughts in spring as the yellow violets bloom
        and the cherry forms its first full buds
the tonic cords along the legs and arms of youth
        and youth passing into maturity, ripening its flesh
growing softer, less unattainable, ruddy and spotted plum

daily, I mistake—there was a medication I forgot to take
there was a man who gave himself, decently, to me & I refused him

in a protracted stillness, I saw that heron I didn't wish to disturb
was clearly a white sack caught in the redbud's limbs

I did not comprehend desire as a deadly force until—
        daylight, don't leave me now, I haven't done with you—
                nor that, in this late hour, we still cannot make peace

if I, inconsequential being that I am, forsake all others
how many others correspondingly forsake this world

       light, light: do not go
I sing you this song and I will sing another as well

Though it was the centerpiece of my book *Chronic,* the poem "chronic"
was nearly the last written for the collection. Perhaps that fact reveals
something about my own process as an artist. I am an *outward-in*
poet as opposed to an *inward-out.* That is to say, I begin with what's on
the surface of things, what's visible, and dive deeper into its interior,
rather than starting in the heart of a matter and reaching outward to
find language to express it. If I were a sculptor I'd be one who works
at subtracting from a block of stone or wood rather than building
upward. So the book itself was always a search for a center, starting
simply with my fascination with the letter *c* and thinking about what
kinds of words start with *c,* what kinds of words end with *c,* and—
eventually—what kinds of words have *c* at the beginning and at the
end. Let me tell you, it's a short list. *Chic* is a good one. I like *chthonic*
but know it's obscure and hard for most people to know how to pro-
nounce. So, when I hit upon *chronic,* I had that definite feeling—like
I had stumbled upon something true about how I saw the world in
this period of my life. I was in a chronic condition: living with an

incurable (but treatable) illness, stuck in an incurable relationship that was destined to end (if only we could end it, which the book helped do), and living in a country chronically addicted to its own unhealthy environmental policies. I thought of *Chronos,* the ancient archetype of time, and understood time itself to be a central dimension of my writing then and now. Not just quantifiable time and how we calendar it. But also time signatures: the beat, the rhythm of language and how poets consider it as something that can impose order and regularity to a line. I have never gone gaga over orderly, symmetrical, persistent, consistent, devoted, regular form. I mean . . . I do admire the well-made. But it is the flawed I fascinate over. What caused the heart to skip here? What caused the breath to falter? When the regimented, ordered world experiences a glitch in the circuitry . . . when the cadence fails to carry out its marching orders . . . well, that's an opportunity for resistance, escape. It's a place where the unreliable and imperfect human heart takes precedence over the mechanical, exact, and empirical sounds of structure, design, alinement, compliance. I am ever refusing to comply or keep order. In short, I resist, at my core, the very idea of perfection or its ugly cousin: oppression. Because even the mind itself can be tricked into thinking that having everything conform to preset rules might be a good thing. Well, maybe in the real world we need patterns, rules, standards. But not in the mind. The mind must still be a wild place where we go to experience the raw, generative, surprising combinations of thoughts that I feel are central to poetry. You have to be willing to overthrow the government of your own imagination. If you can't do that, how can you take charge of your own destiny at those moments that most demand independent and autonomous thinking? To keep regular time within a poem is a form of prosodic tyranny.

I dislike sentences and time for exactly the same reasons—because they include a foregone inevitability. They behave as if there's a beginning, middle, and end to all things. And I for one am not sure that's true. I don't think time is best understood as a flat line and I don't think language is best understood as "a complete thought." Even a book . . . we think of it as having a start and a finish. But in a book of poems, really, you are free to roam around in any order and, for the most part, you aren't going to "lose your place" in a book of poems because you can open up and read wherever you like. Even if the author has given you all sorts of clues that you have to go chronologically . . . you can defy chronology. You can resist time. And you can read without ever reaching the ultimate punctuation mark, the period, that signals something is over. Mind you, I don't feel like I am right about my assessment of time and/or syntax. But I'm not wrong, either. Language is precisely the experimental place where anything can happen. You can actually change verb tenses within a sentence and have the sentence refer to both present and past at the same time. Rhetoric provides some fancy terms for this, such as *anacoluthon,* which basically means "doesn't adhere to conventional expectations of how grammar behaves." Sometimes as we're speaking or writing our focus shifts, and that shift can be captured in real time by the words themselves: "That restaurant where you had the bacon burger let's go there again." "I didn't want to say anything in front of your brother is he still searching for work?" Sometimes we self-interrupt because the train of thought is no longer going to the same destination we set out for: "Darling get your keys and honestly are you going to wear that shirt remember to lock up I love you." Ah, the train of thought . . . I thought I missed it altogether. And then I went back to look at the origin of this poem and discovered something: when I was close to finishing the entire book that "chronic" sits at the center of, I was staying in a barn, on an old blueberry farm, so I could figure out how to make unity out of the pages I had completed thus far. I wrote to a friend about a poem I had been working on:

> the poem had started in California—actually, I started making notes on a train ride from Sacramento to Oakland. Then I finished it here—had thought that it was going to be an abandonment, but it kept calling me back. In the quiet of the countryside I was able to listen to the poem and find it in the dark. Mysterious, the workings of art—I'm still puzzled by how it is that some poems work and some do not.

Sorry. The train of thought was a literal train. I had been making notes each time I would journey through or to the Central Valley of California, a place I had known well as a teen but now lacked connection to. I did not want that connection to end. And yet I did not want to move back to the place at all. I simply wanted to love it from afar. And as I worked through the various notes, I cut away stuff. Horrible lines that were too literal, like:

> death is not something you can club like a seal or pet like a cat
> cannot be unrun
> cannot be stared down, can surprise you with its sudden proximity

Yes, I knew that death was lurking around the edges of this poem. But I did not want it to win. I wanted to stay in the present, uncertainty always abounding, but resilience too . . . surprise . . . joy . . . determination to go on. So how could I end a poem that had, in my mind, no beginning, which started in a middle space and resolved itself in a middle space? The inspiration came from the ancient Homeric Hymns, which would often conclude with promise of more stories, more poems: I sing you this song, and I will sing another as well. I didn't have to worry about whether love or life or planet or terrain was coming to an end. I could stay in it as long as I kept the poem going. And the best way to keep the story (and yourself) alive, you will remember from the tale of Scheherazade, the narrator of most of *The Arabian Nights,* is to promise more to come.

Something About John Coltrane

Something about a tree in shallow sleep
Listening for what it wants to remember:

The note of a seed, its neck sliding through
Dirt and its confusion—nothing cleansed

Of struggle. The weight lost after death,
A confrontation of death. John Coltrane

Even in death is a perfect instrument
Of water and working the day past its zero—

The fires in the trees, a *legless rabbit*
Drifting across the sky—dream of a mule

Covered in crows opened in front of a mule
Covered in crows, their wings beating against him

Like skin. An autumned tree in autumn
Watching fire autumn the other trees.

It doesn't have to make sense now; it can
Make sense later on. A mule covered in crows—

Sometimes, you got to stick a little grass
In your mouth to sound like God. Allow crows.

Something about John Coltrane

Something about the bells in a faun's hair,
A Black boy standing in the rain at the edge

Of the road, wondering how to cross it
Without summoning his death or its hand-

Maidens, the grasshoppers clicking against him
Like he's the water the world has been meaning

To come to—all the world's water trapped inside
Him and needing to be let out. Something

About water waking a ghost, and the ghost
Waking a seed, rain in the hair of the world,

And the world opening its sudden flesh
The way stone opens sound against it—a bridge

Thrown from one absence to another,
As if to say, *Extinction, I can live there too.*

Something about Marion Brown

In a Georgia afternoon, the faun listens
To the Holy Ghost in a trickle of water

And is suddenly thrown down on the floor
Of the Sanctified Church, the woman's feet

Lifting, stomping against the wooden boards,
And God somewhere he ain't supposed to be

Or be momentarily, wasp in the hedge
Sheltering from the rain; a woman's skirt

Hoisted and gladdened above her knee, the hem,
The hem of her garment touched by the faun's eye

And holy, holy, holy is thy name and the snow
The woman becomes on the floor and the water

Ticking against the bottom of the pail, and, Lord,
The bridge opening above the faun in the air,

And he is what memory permits—pine needles
Turning on the skin of a bucket of water,

A bare shoulder in the rain,
God somewhere he ain't supposed to be.

                              Something about Marion Brown

When the light came to the Georgia faun,
It was in a trickle of water, a brown leaf

Suddenly underfoot in the spring's ringing
Green, the leaf underfoot spoke, speaks, became

A ladder of tongues—ghost and the good wood
A house fire needs—*yes, good God, good God yes*—

Became the pleasure of placing your mouth—
Oh yes, Lord, right here, right now Lord—on something

Holy and holding it there until every
Sound in you becomes water—water moving

Over stone, moving in the hair of the trees,
Moving over the breast of the bee, beaver,

Buck of the day, its brown shoulder bearing
The hesitant light, its crown and thorn, water

Moving over the infinite gates of the city,
Moving as the wing of the wasp, which is

The voice of God, water moving over the two
Realms of the body, moving as the name of God—

Something is coming to kill him,
And something is coming to be born.

Today, the faun is both. Something beyond blood.
Wasp somewhere in the hedge sheltering from the rain.

Something about Aretha Franklin

Cousin Mary, don't weep. The eternal
Without the wound of eternity begins now.

Sometimes, you can be made more   than your body
While still in your body. Now, that's power—

A dog suddenly crying in the stables
For no other reason than something lifted

In him in the afternoon, lifted way up
And shook him into a moan and blade of grass

Gathered by a gale wind into a speaking
Thing. Just ask the Georgia faun all caught up

In some running and gladdened by it. Happy
Is what the old folks say. The boy, happy,

Happying in the field with nothing more
Than his body and the dark landing its dark

Against him. It doesn't have to make sense now.
It can make sense later on. The faun coming

In the rain. The dark bending about him.
Power, Cousin Mary, power in the faun

Climbing into the tree as the dark earth flying.
And the clouds coming together above him,

And no danger, no danger to hanging
In the lower heavens as a bell,

As foreign pollen breaking in the wind,
Scattering its brown voice on anything

That will bear and not bear its gold. Vine, fence,
A pail of water, the exposed shoulders of God.

Now, that's power, Cousin Mary. And nothing
Dying rudely or for a dream of the rood.

The dream of this tree is not what will die
In it but what will live upside down

In the rain, trying its voice in heaven
And on earth. Power, eternal power,

Cousin Mary. Don't weep.

Something about the Dream of a Tree

Something about a mule covered in crows,
The mule ridden by a faun with bells in his hair,

And the boy ringing across the field,
And the field ringing across the boy,

And all this ringing opening and with
And full of and tarrying and the silk skin of

And glory and the hem of a garment and *Help me,
Holy Ghost* and *yes, Lord, yes* and *the tiny racket*

A seed makes cracking open in the dark and the stone
In the field worshipping the field by letting

The day fall all about it without moving,
And the dusk riding the rain and the tree

Dreaming and the light, the light without
Confession, castigation or beauty

But beauty, and the faun thrown down
In memory of once watching a hawk

Plucking red coins from the breast of a squirrel,
And the faun mimicking the hawk, his head

Dipping forward in the gesture of prayer,
His mouth working against the wind, the invisible

Breast and belly of an animal and the seed
Of something opening inside him

For which there was no source so call it mercy,
Grace, or nothing   but becoming power.

Prayer. Hawk. The dream of a tree . . .

The dream, also an autopsy—
What came in the middle of the night, a tree

Muttering about the muddle of fragrance,
Wounded sky *bewound in light,* morning

Misted in murder, maggots chattering
Dawn's red rousing, calling it milk,

My Cherie Amour's mystic wobble—
The autopsy, also a dream—what came:

A boy who found his work on the road
And had to lie down there with his work—

The hostility of living between the bullets
And the bullets hanging you against the night,

By the lapel, for examination, for a song,
For the smiths of gold, for gold, for the gallows,

For the fragrance of a field covered in crows
And the crows lifting as if a great black tent

Rising to shield the field from pestilence
But the crows just rising crows, the fragrance

Of freedom but not freedom itself—and here
Silence, what came in the middle of the night—

An autopsy, a dream: a boy on the road,
Crows bowing and bowing and bowing to the dead.

Something about Michael Brown

Something about Mahalia Jackson's wig,
The crow and angel of it, its closer-

Walk-with-Jesus, with-thee, satisfied, lonely,
Holy, ghost, blessed in rapture, actual

And otherwise, her wig, a walking on water
With the faith of a wig; each wave of black hair

A pew strapped to the forehead of prayer
And singing all in it. What's it all about

Is burning beyond loss, learning to rise
In and out of disaster smelling of smoke

That can heal the sick—wild cathedral
In the wilderness opening itself

To any light, dream, or dram of song unhitched
From heaven; and the mules and men get so happy,

Hallelujahed, they strut, brown-suited, bewound
In light like bow-legged Louis Armstrong

At the Newport Jazz Festival, 1970, Mahalia
Lining out ECSTASY and sweating through it

Until it can do nothing but rain
And the second line, confused, leaf-strewn, late

Limps onto stage, but Mahalia Jackson's wig
Keeps flying, and the rain touches evening's brow

Bringing with it the stars and Mahalia
Jackson's wig flying as if a star

Suddenly freed from the mouth of God
A Black tooth blessing. No longer, no longer

Shall you take things second or third hand—joy

Ecstasy, pleasure, the blessing of sitting in the rain
While gathered in the hair of some tree—

Because Mahalia Jackson's wig is flying,
And the dead, for once, are dancing, too—in the rain.

WALKING IN THE RAIN

In writing "Something About John Coltrane," I followed sound—the sound of Alice Coltrane elegizing her husband, John, on harp and piano, the sound of water dripping into a bucket, the sound of the rain, the sound of Mahalia Jackson singing at the Newport Jazz Festival in 1970, the sound of a rock thrown against a tree, the sound of Black folks in a Pentecostal Church speaking in tongues on a Friday evening, the sound of a wasp, the sound of Aretha Franklin weeping through exuberant melisma and vocal runs. I followed the sound of a seed and the sound of the dead leaves that were the seed's offspring. What I hoped to hear in following these sounds, writing toward them, translating and deconstructing them was a type of freedom and inevitability, one that I glimpsed in watching, in attending to each of these sonic events. Freedom and inevitability are for me a playground, the timelessness of art—the ability for something like a poem or a song or a sound to feel as if only that note, only that thing said or expressed could have been what was said. And in saying or expressing the inevitable thing, discovery. The sort of discovery that is also a disappearance. It's the type of discovery and disappearance that I have long studied in the improvisational music of Ornette Coleman and late-career John Coltrane. When I say disappearance, I don't solely mean the author, musician, poet disappearing into the work of art. Rather, I think of disappearing as a type of inevitability reached and expressed. The work of art opens, expands, happens in such a way that what was written, played, or articulated before cannot be returned to or can be returned to only in traces because the work of art has authored and enacted an otherwise—a change—a new sense of time. The work of art, the poem for instance, opens up a new territory such that to go back and rehearse or repeat the same line of the verse is to actually play something, say something that has become extinct. The work of art produces new conditions for being and to tread on old territory feels unsatisfactory, boring, and lifeless. In writing "Something About John Coltrane," I strove for this sort of roaming and territory. However, the striving for this new territory wasn't to plant a flag or declare the aesthetic landscape mine, as so often happens in politics and art. Rather, the purpose was to offer myself beauty—but not the beauty of celebrity, of capitalism's spoils, but the difficult beauty of having to walk home in the rain, of having to find beauty outside of capitalism's spoils. I wanted to offer myself what is not freely given—silence, the freedom to make sense later on (if at all), sound—the ecstasy and ghost of it, the wetness of the rain, dancing with the dead, pleasure, pleasure and more pleasure. I offered myself me but over there. Otherwise and free.

April 17, 1942, Jackie Robinson Gets His First Major League Hit and We Still Us

if you ever stood at the plate
looked out at the mound and saw fang and
the future burned bodies of the first
favorite pastime and a pastlife on
a painful pasture and a pastor telling you
of your birthright of burden
if you knew he was having a ball spitting
your way and had a ball was going low and
going high and to the right whispering
nigger in your ear as it whizzed past
your head better duck better duck better
batter batter bitter changeup but you
knew it wasn't no changeup at all
if you could see the curveball coming
before you got to the game before they
gave you a number and a position before
they trusted you with a bat
and if you ever took a bunt when a home run
was easy but you knew a home run could
easily mean a hard run home

Here is the truth. I was trained as a poet. Studied it in undergrad. But I
don't remember much of what I was taught. However, I do recall some

things, like sitting in class as the singular Black student, which was only ever an issue for me when it came time to workshop.

And it seemed like it was always time to workshop.

Poems passed around. Odes to hats and boots. Trees and wooded bungalows. Teenaged transcendental attempts. Postmodern practice. *Who is the next Ashbery?* Not me. I knew that. Because not only was my approach different, but the tradition from which my interest in poetry was birthed was far from anything we were studying in class.

I wanted to write jazz. And blues. And hip-hop. And country roads. And city streets. And grits. And moonshine. And shit-talk. And how laughter and sex and getting by and getting over are all dancing with the complicated truth of self-preservation in the face of absurd hatred in this country. I wanted to write something Black. Hughes and Baraka and Sanchez and Fauset and Bennett and Brooks and Clifton and Bontemps and on and on and on.

No one knew what I was talking about. They said my work was rudimentary. That it lacked sophistication because it "lacked ambiguity." I'd explain that this tradition—and the people this work has in mind—didn't and, in most accounts, still don't have the luxury of ambiguity. We tend to recognize the potential in language beyond ourselves. Beyond the magic of stanza making. But how language can live in the body. Can live in the mouth. Can steel a backbone. This is why Lucille Clifton's "won't you celebrate with me" is so heavily quoted in the Black community. A mantra for survival. Or why Maya Angelou's "Phenomenal Woman," or Nikki Giovanni's "Ego Tripping" feel like they're owned, not just by the poet, but by every Black girl trudging through that intersectional briar patch. Or why it's so easy for us to just rattle off, "Well, son, I'll tell you: / Life for me ain't been no crystal stair." For me, poetry is meant to communicate something. That something doesn't necessarily have to be an answer. Just a framework of life, whether sliver or chunk.

That being said, this is where "April 17, 1942, Jackie Robinson Gets His First Major League Hit and We Still Us" comes from. Does the poem work? Well, that's up to you. Do the words work? Yes. In many ways. Each line, each word, is in some way mimicking what the people rooted in this tradition have had to do—pull double duty. Lifting more than their fair share, and that's what makes this seemingly simple poem a world to be explored. Maybe it's about racism in the 1940s. Or, maybe it's about Jackie Robinson, the first Black man to play in the major leagues. Or maybe, still, it's about any Black person—perhaps a student—wrestling with being excellent in a space that feels not only foreign but also dangerously dismissive.

Saudade

In the republic of flowers I studied
the secrets of hanging clothes I didn't
know if it was raining or someone
was frying eggs I held the skulls
of words that mean nothing you left
between the hour of the ox and the hour
of the rat I heard the sound of two
braids I watched it rain through
a mirror am I asking to be spared
or am I asking to be spread your body
smelled like cathedrals and I kept
your photo in a bottle of mezcal
semen-salt wolf's teeth you should have
touched my eyes until they blistered
kissed the skin of my instep for thousands
of years sealed honey never spoils
won't crystallize I saw myself snapping
a swan's neck I needed to air out
my eyes the droplets on a spiderweb
and the grace they held who gave me
permission to be this person to drag
my misfortune on this leash made of gold

"Saudade" is a poem I wrote several years ago after I took a solo trip to Portugal. I was going through a divorce at the time, and I was incredibly lonely. Love felt elusive, impossible. When I learned about the meaning of this term on my trip, I was taken aback because it was so familiar to me. I had known this absence my entire life. I wanted what was not possible. My desires were too vast.

The simplest definition of *saudade* is that it's a state of deep longing for someone or something that is absent or never existed. However, it goes far beyond that. It's a word with many layers, a term that is ripe for poets and artists. How do we describe the ache of wanting? How do we embody this singular human restlessness?

They say *saudade* is an impossible word to truly translate, so this poem is only a humble attempt to capture its essence. I'm not Portuguese or Brazilian, so I'm not familiar with its cultural roots and implications. I suppose that what I'm doing here is reaching, which is what I'm doing with all my work. The ineffable fascinates me, so I get as close as I can. The imagery I use here is both disturbing and beautiful because that intersection is essentially my home. The term "republic of flowers" in the beginning of the poem was something I saw on a sign in Lisbon. It was the name of a company, but I don't remember what kind. Flowers? Ice cream? Perfume? I honestly don't want to know. It will ruin the romance of it. When I saw the sign, I gasped and wrote the phrase in my journal because I knew I would eventually use it. It just sounded so perfectly poetic. What a strange juxtaposition, I thought. The image of the frying eggs came to me when I checked into a hotel in Porto, and I literally couldn't tell whether the sound I suddenly heard was frying eggs in the kitchen nearby or a sudden rain pour. It made me think deeply about sounds and how we assign them meaning. Two unrelated things can sound the same.

I'm proud of this poem because it was a real artistic leap for me at the time. The unconventional form was not something I had ever tried. But I wanted to reach beyond what I knew because that's what the poem was asking for. See, I'm the kind of sap that genuinely believes that poems need to reveal themselves to you. All you gotta do is move out of the way.

Omitting punctuation felt necessary because the poem had to feel breathless and rushed. I wanted to mimic the desire itself. I wanted the reader to feel disoriented and uncomfortable. The last image of the misfortune on the leash made of gold is meta in that I was thinking of what it means to be a writer. We're all just dragging our traumas around.

————————————————— Diane Seuss

Still Life with Two Dead Peacocks and a Girl

She comes out of the dark seeking pie, but instead finds two dead peacocks.
One is strung up by its feet. The other lies on its side in a pool
of its own blood. The girl is burdened with curly bangs. A too-small cap.
She wanted pie, not these beautiful birds. Not a small, dusky apple
from a basket of dusky apples. Reach in. Choose a dusky apple.
She sleepwalked to this window, her body led by its hunger for pie.
Instead, this dead beauty, gratuitous. Scalloped green feathers. Gold breast.
Iridescent-eyed plumage, supine on the table. Two gaudy crowns.
She rests her elbows on the stone windowsill. Why not pluck a feather?
Why lean against the gold house of the rich and stare at the bird's dead eye?
The girl must pull the heavy bird into the night and run off with it.
Build a fire on the riverbank. Tear away the beautiful feathers.
Suck scorched, tough, dark meat off of hollow bones. Look at her, ready
    to reach.
She'd hoped for pie. Meringue beaded gold. Art, useless as tits on a boar.

I have been writing poems since I was fourteen years old. I typed them on a manual typewriter. This was in the early 1970s, and the typewriter was old even then, probably from the 1930s. I don't know where it came from and I don't know where it went.

I learned something from every poem I ever wrote, even if it was ill-conceived, cloying, or stupid. When I was eighteen, I learned by writing a poem called "MONSTER WOMAN." The title and many of the words were typed in all caps. "She BIG AND MEAN," it began. "She

206

CRASHIN through the RAZZ-berries. She EAT THE BRAINS of fawns, young quail, ROCK STARS, and RATS . . ." Sort of silly, but from that poem I learned that I could bend language and typography to my own transgressive purposes, that I could invent a self on the page, though in "MONSTER WOMAN" I described that self in the third person. She was one-dimensionally powerful, stalking the landscape. Cartoonish. Green. In writing her, I laid claim to something in myself I hadn't yet enacted in the world. The poem ended this way: "No use RUNNIN. No use bein SCARED, MISTER. Just PUT ON that FOOTBALL HELMET and KISS the good life GOODBYE." I'd never read a poem like that. I don't know why I thought I could write one.

A few decades later, "Still Life with Two Dead Peacocks and a Girl" came to be. Overtly, it seems to have little to do with "MONSTER WOMAN," but it may carry a similarly transgressive tenor, albeit managed very differently. The impetus for the poem was a dream. All I remembered of it, on waking, were the words "STILL LIFE" emblazoned in the dark behind my eyelids. I had always loved visual art—I was an art history minor in college—but I hadn't been particularly drawn to still life painting. But here it was, announcing itself in my dream. I did what all contemporary mystics do with dream information. I googled it. The first painting that came up was Rembrandt's *Still Life with Two Dead Peacocks and a Girl.* I fell in love with the title. Such a fancy bird, but here, dead, ready to be consumed by the eye and the mouth, and then the tagging on of "a girl" at the end—oh, by the way—there's a girl. The painting itself drew me in further. One peacock hangs upside down by its foot from what looks to be a hooked cord. Its wings are splayed, exhibiting the variegations of its feathers. The head hangs upside down, sharp beak in profile. The other peacock rests in a pool of blood upon a counter or table. Behind and between the bodies of the birds is a basket filled with apples. These are the primary elements of still life in the painting: apples, birds, and blood. The painting would not have entered my imagination so deeply without the girl, leaning on her elbows in the windowsill from out of the dark and gazing at the scene, matching us gaze for gaze. Don't we all love looking at dead things?

I had been writing American Sentences, Allen Ginsberg's invention. Ginsberg believed the anglicized three-line haiku (haiku are traditionally written in a single vertical line of seventeen syllables in Japanese) didn't work in English. He thought the more "American" version of the haiku, an offshoot, would be a single seventeen-syllable sentence trekking across the page. It occurred to me that I might somehow respond to the painting in a series of American Sentences. Readers might not pick up on the syllable count, but it would provide me with a compressive practice. Keep me from wandering off the edge of the page. And what if I limited myself to fourteen lines, a kind of sonnet? The syllable-counting became an alternative to meter and rhyme. It offered up another sonic pattern—more syntax than music.

The first line became my guide into the rest of the poem: "She comes out of the dark seeking pie, but instead finds two dead peacocks." Situation, conflict, subject. In writing toward seventeen syllables, I found myself defining the girl in primal observations. She is hungry. She seeks not just any food, but pie. Instead of pie, she gets dead peacocks. She comes out of the dark. She is not of the house. She is outside it, looking in. A peasant. An Other. Then the poem's true subject came sliding in. "She sleepwalked to this window, her body led by its hunger for pie. / Instead, this dead beauty, gratuitous." There is hunger and there is beauty. There is pie and there is peacock. A tension between art that feeds and art that offers us gratuitous beauty. Between "the gold house of the rich" and the people's hunger. And, more personally, between outsider and insider, rural girl and poetry world.

Poems are smarter than I am. Like dreams, they come out of the dark and lead me to uncanny arrivals. The syllable counting, and the fourteen lines and the volta, or turn of thought, that we see in traditional sonnets, distracted my analytical brain enough for the deeper, more mysterious content to ooze up from the cytoplasmic goo. This is where the poem, and the book it would become part of, opened up for me. I was able to see the intersection between the rural, working-class Midwest, where I was raised by a single mother, and still life subject matter—bowls, fruit, kitchen implements. The undervalued realm of women's work. I recognized that pie-seeking girl with her complicated yearning. Then with the volta, the plot of the poem shifts: "The girl must pull the heavy bird into the night and run off with it. / Build a fire on the riverbank. Tear away the beautiful feathers. / Suck scorched, tough, dark meat off of hollow bones. Look at her, ready to reach." I notice, now, the verbs: *pull, run, build, tear, suck, reach.* Anything but still. She must reach in from the dark, break the illusion of the picture plane, build her own fire, and scorch her own bird. It's not what she wants, but it's what she has. Whatever beauty is, she must subsist on its marrow. I knew girls like her. I was and am a girl like her, as is my mother. Not unlike Eve, reaching across the threshold for the forbidden fruit.

The poem's last sentence, "Art, useless as tits on a boar," came to me with the surprise of a slap. "Useless as tits on a boar" was an idiom in my mom's family, originating in her father's barbershop in a village with a dirt main street. "You know Henry," someone might say. "He's useless as tits on a boar." There it was—my mother's voice and point of view. Her irony, her capacity for calling out the bullshit. A MONSTER WOMAN, of a kind. I loved the leap of calling art useless, even in the midst of an artful poem about art. The book that grew up around this first poem explores high art and low culture, the matriarchy of still life, the complexity of stillness. That life, despite its losses, is *still life*. The girl is less monstrous than MONSTER WOMAN, but just as much a trespasser. On Rembrandt, and Ginsberg, and the sonnet itself. Framed by the window, the painting's frame, and the sonnet's inimitable architecture, she looks. She hungers. She plunders and feeds herself.

The Master's House

To wave from the porch
To let go of the grudge
To disrobe
To recall Ethel Rosenberg's green polka-dotted dress
To call your father and say, *I'd forgotten how nice everyone in these red
  states can be*
To hear him say, *Yes, long as you don't move in next door*
To recall every drawn curtain in the apartments you have lived
To find yourself at thirty-three at a vast expanse with nary a papyrus
  of guidance, with nary a voice, a muse, a model
To finally admit out loud then, *I want to go home*
To have a dinner party of intellectuals with a bell, long-armed, lightly-
  tongued, at each setting
To sport your dun gown
To revel in face serums
To be a well-calibrated burn victim to fight the signs of aging
To assure financial health
To be lavender sachets and cedar lining and all the ways the rich might
  hide their rot
To eye the master's bone china
To pour diuretic in his coffee and think this erosive to the state
To disrobe when the agent asks you to
To find a spot on any wall to stare into
To develop the ability to leave an entire nation thusly, just by staring
  at a spot on the wall, as the lead-vested agent names article by
  article what to remove

To do this in order to do the other thing, the wild thing

To say this is my filmdom, The Master's House, and I gaze upon it and
    it is good

To discuss desalination plants and terroir

To date briefly a banker, a lapsed Marxist, and hear him on the phone
    speaking in billions of dollars, its residue over the clear bulbs of his
    eyes, as he turns to look upon your nudity

To fantasize publishing a poem in the *New Yorker* eviscerating his little
    need

To set a bell at each intellectual's table setting ringing idea after idea,
    and be the simple-footed help, rushing to say, *Yes?*

To disrobe when the agent asks you to

To find a spot on any wall to stare into

To develop the ability to leave an entire nation thusly, just by staring
    at a spot on the wall

To say this is my filmdom, The Master's House

To recall the Settler who from behind his mobile phone said, *I'm
    filming you for God*

To recall this sad God, God of the mobile phone camera, God of the
    small black globe and pixelated eye above the blackjack table at
    Harrah's and the metal, toothed pit of Qalandia checkpoint the
    same

To recall the Texan that held a shotgun to your father's chest,
    sending him falling backward, pleading, and the words came to
    him in Farsi

To be jealous of this, his most desperate language

To lament the fact of your lamentations in English, English being
    your first defeat

To finally admit out loud then, *I want to go home*

To stand outside your grandmother's house

To know, for example, that in Farsi the present perfect is called the
    relational past, and is used at times to describe a historic event
    whose effect is still relevant today, transcending the past

To say, for example, *Shah dictator bude-ast* translates to *The Shah was a
    dictator,* but more literally to *The Shah is-was a dictator*

To have a tense of is-was, the residue of it over the clear bulb of your
   eyes
To walk cemetery after cemetery in these States and nary a gravestone
   reading *Solmaz*
To know no nation will be home until one does
To do this in order to do the other thing, the wild thing, though
   you've forgotten what it was

This poem was born, as most of my poems are born, of conversation. A friend, the poet Roger Reeves, was telling me, as I remember, he considers the page a site of freedom, and a poem an enactment of it. We are both devoted to liberation, Reeves and I, and to its life off the page. And yet I wasn't, as I remember, agreeing. I said the page itself is an enclosure. It is a limit, capacious or not, on what can be done. Music, too, and form—all the ways a poem shapes what is said—all these ways, too, are limits.

And so, I said, the poem's real potential is to reveal the enclosures we are subject to. A poem, rather than imagining or enacting a freedom, names its un-freedom. In the most direct language possible, a poem names what simply "is." In the case of "The Master's House," what "is" was not free. This was in 2017, and I was as I often am in these conversations, in a car idling outside an errand I am supposed to run.

"I just thought of a poem," I said. "I have to go." And while I hadn't yet thought of the entirety of this poem, I had thought: I will write a closed poem of endless beginning, re-beginning, that goes nowhere other than compromise. And it would be, as only a poem can be, global and intimate, funny and profane, mournful and ecstatic, a meditation on freedom and complicity pivoting on that most forgiving and greedy rhetorical device: anaphora.

I don't think all poems are made this way. Not all come in a CVS parking lot. Not all capitulate to their repressions and scorn. Not all think of a rhetorical enclosure before they set out. Nor do I wish them to—how terribly boring. But I do believe a poet must know for themself what they are doing and why. What little plot of thought and self and syntax they are devoting themself to. I believe a writer shouldn't shy away from naming the "should" of their writing. Even if it is to trace the ways this should evolves over time. Especially if.

My should, when writing "The Master's House," was simply: every part of a poem should work to name what is. And that has not changed for me.

What has changed, as life devoted to poetry is as the poem itself devoted to repetition and change, is what I understand as "is." In "The Master's House," the "is" is the observable, the verifiable world. On this October morning in 2021, I am not so sure anymore. There is a thing that shimmers behind the observable, a thing that poetry scratches at naming, and that's what I find myself moving toward now.

Of course, deep attention, to the observable and the otherwise, got me there. And that is what I will follow. And that attention will reveal to me what the poem will need to be, and the needs of the poem will then alter my gaze a bit so that I will find more to feed the poem—and like that, back and forth, I set out.

Put another way: Years after I wrote "The Master's House," in the thick of editing an evasive poem in the middle of the lockdown of the pandemic, I dreamed. In this dream, I complained to someone about not knowing what to do with this troublesome poem. This person said, "Well, if you want to write richer poems, you will have to live more richly."

"The Master's House" and its relentless pointing to paucity and compromise led me there. Because I don't want to write the same poem again and again, I had to change my life. That was the poem's charge. That's the charge of poetry, I'd say—the breaths taken after the words are spoken, changing the air.

A Handbook of Poetic Forms

I use acrostics to get laid
Then pulp to pay my rent
And ballads to buy off the Christians
Sonnets to learn counterfeit
Chant to reverse dark circles
Cantos trigger insanity and worse
Terza rima when I feel like swimming laps
Odes for luck in blackjack
Index for sedative
A prayer to form searchlights
Haiku to throw a shadow and tear it in half
A diary to become more gay
Pantoums to pace the cave paintings
Limerick to lock a private room
Blues to light my face in a fedora
Rap to have my postures blown out
Lyric to form my shaving mirror
Sestinas to map my double life

I wrote this poem largely to amuse myself. I stole the title and concept from a book on teaching poetry edited by Ron Padgett. The book is organized as an encyclopedia of poetic form. Each of the forms is presented in alphabetical order. It has the feel and design of a manual. The overall arrangement seemed to imply that one could "master" poetry if they carefully worked their way through this book. That bit of delusional thinking reminded me immediately of Ezra Pound's *ABC of Reading* and the hilarious, bossy tone of that text.

During the writing, it felt as though I were in collaboration with another writer. It was like I was throwing out the first half of the line and then this disembodied second voice would chime in to complete it and get all the laughs. This piece can also be seen as a meditation on being a working poet and constantly being asked to rearticulate my formal concerns and strategies. It pokes fun at that very literal and often serious question, what is the *use* of writing poetry?

The success of this poem was dependent on keeping the grain of wit alive within the line and then disguising its approach. The tone of voice is made to dart from hope to alarm to annoyance to enchantment. As I reread the poem now, trying to fasten onto aspects of its composition, I find myself instead asking further questions. What is it about the containment of the sonnet that borders on the art of forgery? Why is a shaving mirror upheld as a talismanic object? There is a certain degree of accuracy maintained in these descriptions even at their most abstract. For example, the gait of the pantoum *does* resemble sets of frantic footprints, and the supreme aerial views offered by the sestina do cross over into the realm of cartography.

I don't remember this poem requiring much editing. This is largely the way it first slipped out. I wanted to remain faithful to how the line would lurch, connect, and then rest momentarily. The few lines that I ended up crossing out were the least humorous ones. These sacred forms of poetry are being lined up, crushed and thus relieved of their essence. The residual smoke always flows over into the framing of the next line. I could not have written a poem filled with punch lines had I not used the rhythm of the list to guide my voice along.

The answers that flow out from this poem then lure us into devotional thinking, that poetry could possibly form a field of protection around the writer or even the reader. The act of listing can uncover a deceptively simple side entrance into the poem where luminous details emerge without any fear of self-consciousness. It's as though we have surrendered ourselves to the grip of the line, the warp that binds us between sense and sound.

I consider "A Handbook of Poetic Forms" a personal best because the fragile charm and surprise of the poem are maintained over eighteen lines. It runs slightly longer than a traditional sonnet but does achieve a similar cradling effect. A lot of my other work breaks immediately into fragmentation and collage, the line breaks are terse, and the page is often treated as a literal score. This poem came out in a much easier fashion. The rhythm of the lines felt open and continuous, as though I were eavesdropping in a very still room with the light falling just right. I am proud to have turned a series of private jokes into poetic matter.

Jake Skeets

Maar

buffaloburr veins around siltstone
mounds on the monocline

flow rock smooths over into oar
cutleaf cornflower overgrown

pollen blown out
larkspur and beeplant on the meadow

grasp at the basement fault
taut atop diatreme

bulb liquid overflows into grasses
yellow sheen in the winds

laccolith ghost shadows over hungry dust
rains chew down medicine twigs

blue flax left as moans
that foam into the sky

numb star erect over the horizon
burning bomb quiet as stone

How to Read This Poem

There are many discussions about how "difficult" or "cryptic" a poem can be. Many poets and writers will discuss the lyric, the narrative, the imagistic, the sentimental. Often, the phrase "Show, don't tell" will make its rounds in these discussions. Showing is the belief that poems should allow the reader to fully realize the sensory details of a poem. However, telling is often the most urgent urge for a poet or speaker. The desire to tell our stories is a universal feeling. That is the power of language, after all: the movement, the push, the atmospheric pressures that forge the storms in our mouths. How often are we so inspired that we have no choice but to tell, to speak, to scream at the top of our lungs because we simply cannot hold it in? How often are we so surprised that we are actually *speech*less? Our minds are involved in a business of expression. This task is informed by the systems of memories and knowledge construction within the mind itself. Language, then, is not as straightforward as showing or telling. Instead, language is informed by the movement of the world and universe around us. It makes sense that our first attempts at a written language used the earth as the medium.

I'm not interested so much in the argument for or against the idea of telling or showing in a poem. I'm more interested in the argument of the gravitational pull, the invisible force, the organic form that, as the poet Denise Levertov says, brings us to speech. I hypothesized often that the land and universe often trigger memories, images, and fragments of language that build over time and mingle with the experiences we gather inside our minds. The static electricity that builds as a result is the invisible force that informs, shapes, and molds the language we use to express ourselves. The poem, then, is a translation of the land and universe around us. How do we see this play out in a poem? How do we use this hypothesis to "read" poems?

In "Maar," I attempted to test this hypothesis by writing a narrative-driven poem about the volcanic history and landscape of New Mexico. I wrote about the appearance, the composition, and the importance within Navajo creation stories. Then, in revision, I randomized the words using an online word-scramble generator that forced me to move away from the narrative and focus on sounds and images. What images were created as a result of the words ricocheting off each other, collapsing in on each other, and shifting like tectonic plates? What sounds were created by the rumbling, the enjambing, the quaking? So often "Maar" is seen as a poem that is not as readable as other poems because there is no clear narrative. This poem is doing too much showing, perhaps, and not enough telling. There is a landscape and environment, however. The poem mirrors the shifting history of volcanoes, rocks, and deep time in New Mexico. It resembles a field of volcanic rock, maars, and high desert.

I conclude that the energy of the earth brewing beneath our feet found its way into "Maar" through the words themselves, and that is why I love it so much. Though there is no one way to read "Maar," there are the images to witness and sounds to experience. I imagine my readers walking into a volcanic landscape in New Mexico when they read "Maar," even if not explicitly told or shown within the work. I think that's why this is one of my favorite pieces and one I wish would be analyzed more. It avoids the argument of showing versus telling and focuses on the landscape itself. It shifts its breath to the field. And if you've ever walked into a field, you rarely ask yourself: "What does this field mean?" We rarely question whether the field is showing or telling, imagistic or sentimental, lyric or narrative-driven. Instead, we experience the field. We ought to "read" poems similarly; we should experience them first.

— Danez Smith

waiting on you to die so i can be myself

a thousand years of daughters, then me.
what else could i have learned to be?

girl after girl after giving herself to herself
one long ring-shout name, monarchy of copper

& coal shoulders. the body too is a garment.
i learn this best from the snake angulating

out of her pork-rind dress. i crawl out of myself
into myself, take refuge where i flee.

once, i snatched my heart out like a track
& found not a heart, but two girls forever

playing slide on a porch in my chest.
who knows how they keep count

they could be a single girl doubled
& joined at the hands. i'm stalling.

i want to say something without saying it
but there's no time. i'm waiting for a few folks

i love dearly to die so i can be myself.
please don't make me say who.

bitch, the garments i'd buy if my baby
wasn't alive. if they woke up at their wake

they might not recognize that woman
in the front making all that noise.

ON "WAITING ON YOU TO DIE SO I CAN BE MYSELF"

My most popular poem took me thirty minutes to write sitting in a
Michigan airport. Sometimes I feel a way about it, the poem most
taught/most anthologized/most asked for at readings took so little,
came on such a whim. When I perform said poem in public, yes it gets
great cheers and laughs, a few folks might even cry, but I've come to
think it's easy, or easier, to get people to hoot and holler and weep.
What makes an audience stone quiet? What calms all noise and brings
a group of people into a singular focus? What makes them not feel
boisterous but fragile? What can a poem do that takes the wind out of
people?

   This poem took the wind out of me. It took about five years to get
this poem right. I think it's my best because it took the best of me to
find it: my best listening, my best patience, my best sound, best mind.
The only thing that remained consistent was the title, "waiting on you
to die so i can be myself." It was a seed of truth I spent draft after draft
refusing to water with honesty. The idea for the poem was simple
enough: What is it like to love someone you can't be yourself around?
What is it to intentionally remain within the boundaries of someone's
conditional love? Can love for family and a desire for yourself coexist?
What is it to wish for a death you hope to never see? Okay, maybe not
simple, but clear to me from the poem's inception.

   Though clear, I spent many drafts running away from the chilling
simplicity of the answers to those questions, which are not answers
but maybe admittances, confessions, an honesty somewhere outside
of logic. I think those younger selves writing early drafts of this poem

were trying to go for flash, trying to use sound and image to come out of the poem somehow free of the weight of that title, free from the feeling of being locked out of yourself in order to be held by blood relations. I remember one version had me dancing on my beloved's grave, my grief giving way to a gender ecstasy, a celebration of self. What a wicked draft that was. What a false freedom and tainted celebration that poem sought.

It was later in the poem's life—a little further from the clarity and resolution often sought for in spoken word, a little more comfortable being quiet in a poem—that this draft started to come to be. It's a poem made of Black girl things, of hand games and snatched weaves, the beauty of a bare shoulder and the crackle of skins, of Eve and churches and tears, a poem I hope honors the beauty of the women I come from, but also makes room for my place among them, a poem that expects their passing but doesn't call for it. It's a poem without an answer, a poem that simply says what it must.

I see this poem as a compass to the work I'm writing after it. In it, I think I find a voice that wasn't possible when writing my first two collections, a voice that even stands out from the work in the collection it appears in. Its music is not a drum like so much of my work, but a softer tone, more a hand to the thigh keeping time. Its images are right on the money for me, images that collect from looking at and loving on Black folks, images that make me and hopefully my most urgently thought-of readers at home. Maybe what makes it my best is nothing about its product, but about its process. This poem, like other poems I considered for this anthology, took its time and demanded I become a better writer in order to get it right. To encounter questions and ideas that stun my making and shock me out of language is a blessing, and from this poem, I'm learning to make every poem or project such an occasion. Let me slow down my language, let me be dissatisfied with what first comes, let me find the poem that answers to no one, that sings not for the high notes but for the deep, earthy truths.

Sweet Daddy

62. You would have been 62.
I would have given you a Roosevelt Road
kinda time, an all-night jam in a
twine time joint, where you could have
taken over the mike
and crooned a couple.

The place be all blue light
and JB air
and big-legged women
giggling at the way
you spit tobacco into the sound system,
showing up some dime-store howler
with his pink car
pulled right up to the door outside.

You would have been 62.
And the smoke would have bounced
right off the top of your head,
like good preachin'.
I can see you now,
twirling those thin hips,
growling 'bout if it wasn't for bad luck
you wouldn't have no luck at all.
I said,

wasn't for bad luck,
no luck at all.

Nobody ever accused you
of walking the paradise line.
You could suck Luckies
and line your mind with rubbing alcohol
if that's what the night called for,
but Lord, you could cry foul
while B.B. growled Lucille from the jukebox,
you could dance like killing roaches
and kiss the downsouth ladies
on fatback mouths. Ooooweee, they'd say,
that sweet man sho' knows how deep my well goes.
And I bet you did, daddy,
I bet you did.

But hey, here's to just another number—
to a man who wrote poems on the back
of cocktail napkins and brought them home
to his daughter who'd written her rhymes
under blankets.
Here's to a strain on the caseload.
Here's to the fat bullet
that left its warm chamber
to find you.
Here's to the miracles
that spilled from your head
and melted into the air
like jazz.

The carpet had to be destroyed.
And your collected works
on aging, yellowed twists of napkin

can't bring you back.
B.B. wail and blue Lucille
can't bring you back.
A daughter who grew to write screams
can't bring you back.

But a room
just like this one,
which suddenly seems to fill
with the dread odors of whiskey and smoke,
can bring you here
as close as my breathing.

But the moment is hollow.
It stinks.
It stinks sweet.

I was sure that people had grown weary of all my syrupy, teary-eyed babbling about my father. There he was, dead center in everything I read, penned, or spoke aloud—all poems were about him, dedicated to him, or punctuated with his Arkansas gravel, snippets of brown liquor language or the stumbling tenderness with which he raised his one and only baby girl.

When I glimpse my father, it's as if through a murky perfumed mist, a mist blaring that potent swirl of Old Spice and smoke from the blazed end of a Lucky Strike, a fog that occasionally sweet-stinks of scrubbed chitterlings and a whole lotta shot glasses worth of JB. Daddy was a saint in a Kangol, my griot and guide, flawed in just the ways he needed to be in order to father a kid who was gangly, pimpled, painfully nerdish, forever in search of story. Otis Douglas Smith was a lot of things good and a few things bad, but above all he was story. He told himself to me.

And I loved every word of him.

I suppose, for contrast's sake, I should say a word or two about my mother: I inconvenienced her. My birth ruined her body. I was too black. My nose was too wide. My hair crackled as Woolworth's fifty-cent plastic combs died on their way through. There. That's thirty words.

When I confessed to both parents that I wanted to be a writer, my mother sniffed her patented sniff and said, "Only white men do that." Considering the way she walked through the world—wary and beholding, ready to bend in case a white glance swept her way—what she warned was completely true. My father would pull me aside—far, far aside, 'cause he was no fool—to whisper, "You can do any damned thing you want." (The "damned" thrilled my little ears—it was simply the bestest brown liquor language.)

I'm not sure how they ever got together in the first place. My pious mother spoke frequently to Jesus, who told her to stop wearing pants. My father loved card games, gutbucket blues, and the occasional rose-lipped woman poured into a pencil skirt. My parents broke apart, my father moved out, my hair fell out, I cried through fifth grade.

But even though he'd left, my father dared the space every day. While my mother sucked her teeth and watched *Bonanza,* daddy came over after I got home from school and stayed to tuck me into bed with a story—one he made up about people we knew, the people he worked with at the candy factory, the people who populated our chaotic West Side street. I learned that everything was either the beginning or the middle or the ending of story.

Time passed. I saw my father all the time. I grew up. I had a child of my own. (Guess who loved being a grandfather?) Again, I said I wanted to be a writer. No one said no. Together, daddy and I had worn my mother down. She had handed us both over to Jesus.

Here I'll make a long story short, but I'll also make it horrible. A man killed my daddy in a robbery. A bullet burst open the back of my father's head. Because of that day, I am still a changed child. I was twenty-two years old. A changed child.

I truly believe that I strove to call myself "poet" so that I would somehow be qualified to write about the loss of my father. But when I wrote "Sweet Daddy," I didn't know much of anything about poetry. It was from my first book, *Life According to Motown,* one of the initial offerings from Luis Rodriguez's Tia Chucha Press; the book came about because I was a regular at the Green Mill and other Chicago performance spaces, and Luis had asked that terrifying question: "Do you have a manuscript?" and I said yes then though the answer was no.

I hadn't studied poetry with anyone, didn't know who I was supposed to be reading, didn't know an iamb from an amphibrach. I wasn't familiar with the elegance that elegy could be, and I didn't know how the right words could reintroduce a gone body to breath.

But I did know hurt. Hurt was all over me. And I suspected that a poem was something I could read again and again, until, hopefully, the hurt turned to ache, then to memory. Now I know that never happens, not that way.

Why do I feel that "Sweet Daddy" (winner of some contest somewhere for the world's worst poem title) should be anthologized to the ends of the earth? Why did it appear, upon my command, unchanged, in my first *three* books?

It is by no means a notable poem. There's no technical flourish, no lyrical surprise. It's often trite, as poems are when their purpose is to pierce the thick muscle of grief. The poet in me cringes at the casual cluelessness of the line breaks, the clumsy flirtations with cliché. Then there's "And the smoke would have bounced / right off the top of your head, / like good preachin'." What? *What?* In what world do boisterous Baptist sermons bounce off the *tops of heads*? What was I thinking?

And oh, how I wish I hadn't used the word *jazz.* It smacks flat and trendy, there on that line almost by itself, with the arrow of *I'm important* pointing to it. Just. No.

Obviously I don't want this poem exhaustively anthologized because it's good and should be recognized as such. I want it everywhere because after "You can do any damned thing you want," my father never got to see or hear a single poem I'd written. He didn't get to see the rickety stages, the packed barrooms, the classrooms and the buzzing auditoriums with everyone's focus on a changed child telling the story of her father.

I'm a poet, which means I'm a hopeful fool. So I think if this poem were written loudly enough, if it found its way to the pages of a thousand books, my father just might hear how his story ends.

Sleepers

A black-chinned hummingbird lands
on a metal wire and rests for five seconds;
for five seconds, a pianist lowers his head
and rests his hands on the keys;

a man bathes where irrigation water
forms a pool before it drains into the river;
a mechanic untwists a plug, and engine oil
drains into a bucket; for five seconds,

I smell peppermint through an open window,
recall where a wild leaf grazed your skin;
here touch comes before sight; holding you,
I recall, across a canal, the sounds of men

laying cuttlefish on ice at first light;
before first light, physical contact,
our hearts beating, patter of female rain
on the roof; as the hummingbird

whirs out of sight, the gears of a clock
mesh at varying speeds; we hear
a series of ostinato notes and are not tied
to our bodies' weight on earth.

ON "SLEEPERS"

One morning I happened to see a black-chinned hummingbird land on a metal fence. In flight, hummingbirds may beat their wings fifty times a second, and to see one stay still seemed like the longest time. I started to play in language, and the suspense of the still hummingbird led me to the moment when a pianist lowers his head but does not yet touch the keys. And the lowering motion led me to the image of a homeless man who bathes in irrigation water where the water forms a natural pool before it flows into the Santa Fe River. That downward motion also led me to the image of a mechanic draining engine oil out of a car. I mention these details as if they are causally linked. They are not. In writing, I trusted the sound and rhythm, the repeating motion of "for five seconds," and let what happened in my writing happen.

If I write a poem and know where the poem is headed, I find those poems usually don't have deep and essential surprise, and the urgency, that poetry needs. So I often have to shed all notion of what I think the poem wants to say or where it wants to take me. In playing with musical phrases and images, I find a poem can emerge or coalesce without my knowing what it is about. There's a tension between wanting to be in control—I am after all choosing words and shaping the language—and also letting go and being carried into the unknown. In "Sleepers"—I can only say this in hindsight—I notice that the smell of "peppermint through an open window" triggers a memory, then another memory. And in the dark, "touch comes before sight." In this situation, the lovers, though sleeping, are also connected, through physical contact, through an awareness of their hearts beating, and through the sound of a gentle rain on the roof.

The poem takes place in the interval between when the hummingbird lands and when it takes off. And in that space, rather than one space, there are synchronous spaces. Carl Jung once asserted that "synchronicity takes the coincidence of events in space and time as meaning something more than mere chance," and that is what is happening here. In one space, there's a hint of environmental pollution: what will the mechanic do with the used engine oil? Surely he won't dump it down a sewer or pour it into a stream? And gravity, with two meanings, enters the poem with force. Though this poem has a light touch, I hope it has gravitas, a seriousness of purpose and dignity of tone. And, yes, gravity, in its scientific meaning, is an active force. The irrigation water that flows downhill obeys gravity; the engine oil that drains out of the bottom of a car obeys gravity. Yet, when the pianist (obeys gravity and?) finally hits the keyboard with his fingers and starts to play, a series of persistent notes come out, and that ensuing music somehow affirms that the sleeping lovers are not constrained, like mere objects or weights, to the pull of Earth's gravity. In the way that this poem combines sensuous detail, complexity of experience, and braids the natural, human, and erotic, I believe "Sleepers" is representative of my work at this particular moment.

Finally, just as the gears of a clock have different sizes and speeds but work in unison to track time and move the second, minute, and hour hands of a clock, the different phrases in this poem, some shorter, some longer, work in unison. The poem is linguistically one sentence. There are commas, there are semicolons; each phrase works like the gear of a mysterious clock to reveal the inner workings of emotion and consciousness.

The Lushness of It

It's not that the octopus wouldn't love you—
not that it wouldn't reach for you
with each of its tapering arms.

You'd be as good as anyone, I think,
to an octopus. But the creatures of the sea,
like the sea, don't think

about themselves, or you. Keep on floating there,
cradled, unable to burn. Abandon
yourself to the sway, the ruffled eddies, abandon

your heavy legs to the floating meadows
      of seaweed and feel
           the bloom of phytoplankton, spindrift, sea
        spray, barnacles. In the dark benthic realm, the slippery nekton
glide over the abyssal plains and as you float you can feel
                  that upwelling of cold, deep water touch
      the skin stretched over
           your spine. No, it's not that the octopus
                wouldn't love you. If it touched,

if it tasted you, each of its three
hearts would turn red.

Will theologians of any confession refute me?
Not the bluecap salmon. Not its dotted head.

ON "THE LUSHNESS OF IT"

This poem started the way most of my poems do. Some words were
turning over in my mind, and I was listening. I was missing the ocean,
thinking of words connected to its life and depths—*benthic, nekton,
abyssal*—and I followed them.

I try to give myself permission to write out of nothing other than an
interest in listening. I take it on faith that writing poems might help me
cultivate that skill. My interest isn't abstract. I've spent much of my life
witnessing people I love listen just enough to collect evidence to jus-
tify their hardened understandings of one another. Or so it's seemed
to me. What I know more certainly is how often I have found myself
falling—easily, thoughtlessly—into hearing just what I expect to.

Unable to step into the ocean, I entered my vocabulary for what
can be found there. I let myself drift slowly toward this conjuring, an
address to a vertebrate among invertebrates. I let myself drift away
from language in which I heard overt preference for the human, to
imagine a world in which no one is accused of "having no backbone."
I drifted away from words like *invertebrate,* a word that defines most
of the species on earth by what they lack. And somehow I came to
the word *love*—and I was bothered by the feeling that it didn't belong
there.

I know it's hard to perceive what one isn't prepared to perceive.
Here, I was trying to take a step toward the beyond-human world by
paying attention to my language for it—and then trying to loosen it,
enlarge it, make it suppler, more prepared to hold what I don't under-
stand. I feel, in this poem, my language imagination pressing back
against the constrictions of the theologies that shaped me, against the
ways these theologies shaped ideas about love as I once received them.
There have been times that claims of love came to me—inaccurate,

deceptive—when its syllable sounded like the click of being locked inside myself. By letting the word enter a space where I didn't expect it, this poem helped restore for me (and it is a word I need) the word's capacity, vitality, its deep sense of mystery connected all at once to the comic, the ridiculous, to ambivalence, and to danger.

Speaking, for me, has never come easily. The act has been fraught with anxiety of an intensity and weight for which I can't account. But it's when I have language that feels like it can hold something real, or at least alive, that speaking feels possible. I have no claims to make about love, but in this poem it feels good to enter a voice that claims the authority to make claims. I like the sound of its confidence, its defiance, and the way they turn outward and reach toward someone. I like that it doesn't speak out of fear.

An octopus can change texture, shape, color, and the patterns on its skin in a fraction of a second. It eludes its predators through tricks and disguises, one moment taking on the look of a rock, then a lionfish, a sea snake, a reflected cloud moving across water. Its ability to invent ways to transform itself seems intimately connected to its sensitivity to its world, its abilities to taste and in some way *see* with its skin, to intensely perceive what it seems to become. "We become what we love and who we love shapes what we become," instructs Ilia Delio. *Love* comes from the Old English *lufian,* "to cherish; delight in, approve." The octopus awes me for the way it is made to be exquisitely open to touch, but it isn't afraid of solitude. It chooses it.

Sometimes, when you are lucky, a poem you send into the world returns to you in a new way. That happened when a sumptuous performance of "The Lushness of It" briefly appeared online. I don't know the name of its performer, but I remember the red glitter of their gown, and how they introduced "The Lushness of It" as a poem "about being alone with love." That feels true to me. I still feel this poem offering me permission to enjoy that particular aloneness. There's also this: I had no special fondness for octopuses before I wrote it. Now I want them to live through another half billion years, free to love or not love the taste of what they touch.

Ocean Vuong

Not Even

Hey.

I used to be a fag now I'm a checkbox.

The pen tip jabbed in my back, I feel the mark of progress.

I will not dance alone in the municipal graveyard at midnight, blasting sad songs on my phone, for nothing.

I promise you, I was here. I felt things that made death so large it was indistinguishable from air—and I went on destroying inside it like wind in a storm.

The way Lil Peep says *I'll be back in the mornin'* when you know how it ends.

The way I kept dancing when the song was over, because it freed me.

The way the streetlight blinks twice, before waking up for its night shift, like we do.

The way we look up and whisper *Sorry* to each other, the boy and I, when there's teeth.

When there's always teeth, on purpose.

When I threw myself into gravity and made it work. Ha.

I made it out by the skin of my griefs.

I used to be a fag now I'm lit. Ha.

Once, at a party set on a rooftop in Brooklyn for an "artsy vibe," a young woman said, sipping her drink, *You're so lucky. You're gay plus you get to write about war and stuff. I'm just white.* [Pause] *I got nothing.* [Laughter, glasses clinking]

Because everyone knows yellow pain, pressed into American letters, turns to gold.

Our sorrow Midas touched. Napalm with a rainbow afterglow.

Unlike feelings, blood gets realer when you feel it.

I'm trying to be real but it costs too much.

They say the earth spins and that's why we fall but everyone knows it's the music.

It's been proven difficult to dance to machine-gun fire.

Still, my people made a rhythm this way. A way.

My people, so still, in the photographs, as corpses.

My failure was that I got used to it. I looked at us, mangled under the *Time* photographer's shadow, and stopped thinking, *get up, get up.*

I saw the graveyard steam in the pinkish dawn and knew the dead were still breathing. Ha.

If they come for me, take me out.

What if it wasn't the crash that made us, but the debris?

What if it was meant this way: the mother, the lexicon, the line of cocaine on the mohawked boy's collarbone in an East Village sublet in 2007?

What's wrong with me, Doc? There must be a pill for this.

Because the fairy tales were right. You'll need sorcery to make it out of here.

Long ago, in another life, on an Amtrak through Iowa, I saw, for a few blurred seconds, a man standing in the middle of a field of winter grass, hands at his sides, back to me, all of him stopped there save for his hair scraped by low wind.

When the countryside resumed its wash of gray wheat, tractors, gutted barns, black sycamores in herdless pastures, I started to cry. I put my copy of Didion's *The White Album* down and folded a new dark around my head.

The woman beside me stroked my back, saying, in a midwestern accent that wobbled with tenderness, *Go on son. You get that out now. No shame in breakin' open. You get that out and I'll fetch us some tea.* Which made me lose it even more.

She came back with Lipton in paper cups, her eyes nowhere blue and there. She was silent all the way to Missoula, where she got off and said, patting my knee, *God is good. God is good.*

I can say it was gorgeous now, my harm, because it belonged to no one else.

To be a dam for damage. My shittyness will not enter the world, I thought, and quickly became my own hero.

Do you know how many hours I've wasted watching straight boys play video games?

Enough.

Time is a mother.

Lest we forget, a morgue is also a community center.

In my language, the one I recall now only by closing my eyes, the word for *love* is *Yêu.*

And the word for *weakness* is *Yếu.*

How you say what you mean changes what you say.

Some call this prayer, I call it watch your mouth.

Rose, I whispered as they zipped my mother in her body bag, *get out of there.*

Your plants are dying.

Enough is enough.

Time is a motherfucker, I said to the gravestones, alive,
absurd.

Body, doorway that you are, be more than what I'll pass
through.

Stillness. That's what it was.

The man in the field in the red sweater, he was so still
he became, somehow, more true, like a knife wound in a
landscape painting.

Like him, I caved.

I caved and decided it will be joy from now on. Then
everything opened. The lights blazed around me into a
white weather

and I was lifted, wet and bloody, out of my mother, into the
world, screaming

and enough.

NOTES ON "NOT EVEN"

For as long as I can remember, I wanted to begin a poem with the word
hey. Over a decade ago, when I was a younger poet terrified of getting
poetry "wrong," it felt blasphemous to even think about. But there was
something about that casual greeting of "hey" that I think all poets,
in one way or another, have wanted to say, have in fact *been* saying all
along.

In the twelve years I've been writing, this greeting has become a perennial thesis for me: to speak to an unseen person on the other side of the page, the reader's face so close to the words yet always out of view, that a simple "hey" can suddenly feel like a beam of sound shot across the silences of our species. The power of the lyric poem, in this sense, is its very ability to disrupt time without the cumbersome setup of plot or character; it is, itself, utterance, a "hey" amid the cacophonous chatter.

Still, for a long time I was too timid to commit to it. How embarrassing to admit! A so-called poet afraid of saying "hey," such a little word after all. Dozens of times I wrote "hey" into my notebook only to erase it, blushing. How dare I sully Mount Parnassus with such a trite, pedestrian word, a word I have heard so often among friends, even strangers across subway cars in New York or while passing each other on brownstone streets at dusk when, between two men, the word *hey* becomes a pebble tossed into the lake in which all ripples lead to some brief and unwarranted bodily pleasure, seemingly stolen yet somehow long overdue, even earned.

The more I read, however, the more I realized how "safe," Puritan, a word like *hey* in a poem can be among the radical shifts in language breached by elders in lyric traditions across the world. But that's the thing about being a young writer: to realize what is new to you, what is brave even, daring, seemingly impossible, was also the dream (often already achieved somewhere in the archives) of a stranger you will never know but whose linguistic residue you can now touch. And, discovering it, you decide to be even bolder than before, you realize *hey* is just one small horizon among many more. And you start to walk on your own terms. Words are steps, you decide, moving forward.

All this is to say I truly don't know if this poem is my personal best— only that it's the clearest marker of my growth. Using the notebook log as a frame, I hope to dignify the format of the journal, diary, or daybook—mediums often canonically dismissed as subordinate to "real literature" yet vital schemas for Queer folks, and many of us who sing in the dark, where the journal becomes a place to hold portions of ourselves that even our loved ones, parents, sisters, pastors, teachers, might never know. I wanted the mode of the list to garner nonsequitous surprise, the oscillation between the banal and the sublime, the whimsical and the horrific, to have a reified place in my poems the way the sonnet and the pantoum often do in the rest of the genre.

My only regret is that it took so long to say "hey." So I hope you find permission, if you feel so compelled, to say it right away.

The next time you sit down to start a poem, please say "hey" to it for me?

Greenacre

Annuit coeptis

But what if a given surface is coaxed into fruitfulness wrongfully?

For instance, this lushly verdant plain. Imagine it dialed back to feature-lessness, each spiraling stalk retracted, each filigree rosette slow-blinking shut. Dialed back to bare promise, to smooth-napped expanse—the forehead of an alien princess might convey such tranquility: she surveys her ranks of suitors, shakes her exquisite green head, in scarcely feigned regret.

So thinks Cadmus—hand still outstretched in a nation-building gesture—as if to freeze in time this instant: scatter of seeds still aloft, arrayed like little dive bombers in formation.

Not yet puncturing the land.
Not yet rooting, not yet sending up terribly thin, ambitious tendrils toward the light.
Not yet trained onto wire-frame espaliers, not yet combed into bombastic pompadours, not yet extruding seed-pods resembling pale grapes, resembling pearls.

The root of "remorse" isn't *tooth*—he recalls, abruptly—but *to bite*, and then stoops, groping for the biggest rock he can find.

On "Greenacre"

When a poem is still at the front of my mind even years after I've published it, it's sometimes because I feel like I've left something undone—like leaving the house but obsessing over whether you've left the oven on. I can't remember now why I first set out to write a poem about a one-dollar bill. Not the front of the bill, which gets all the attention, but the back of the bill with its trippy landscape of cresting waves and spiderwebs and an inexplicable pyramid surmounted by an equally inexplicable all-seeing eye (apparently a symbol of Freemasonry). To stare at this landscape—to really look at it—is to be immersed in a kind of baroque extravaganza of excess—every square millimeter of surface area is sprouting something, spawning something, spiraling off into greater elaborations, as if you had sprayed your lawn with radioactive fertilizer. A capitalist fantasia of productivity on steroids—or so it seemed to me.

At the time, I was in the middle of writing my book *Blackacre,* which deals with infertility—both the societal shame that surrounds it and my personal experience. Injected with hormones, suffused with other people's expectations, I felt like it would be a failure to remain barren, even as the green field of the dollar is not permitted to be fallow but must produce, must reproduce itself under the demands of capitalism. I imagined a woman—the greenness of the dollar suggested an alien princess—facing the pressure to marry, to bear children, and I thought of her finding the courage to refuse this dictate, at least for a time. To stare too long at the propagating field of the dollar bill is to find yourself longing for blankness, for open space. I thought of what it would be to go back in time to the land prior to human intervention, prior to cultivation, prior to civilization.

The figure of Cadmus, from Greek mythology, came to mind. Cadmus has always interested me—he's an immigrant, actually an Asian immigrant, from what is now Lebanon. He comes to Greece in search of his sister, Europa, who was abducted and raped by Zeus, in the form of a white bull. He never finds his sister, and consults the oracle at

Delphi, who tells him to stop searching for his sister but instead to found a city where a cow, who bears a half-moon mark, stops to rest. At that spot, a dragon attacks and kills his companions. Cadmus manages to kill the dragon, and the goddess Athena advises him to sow the seeds in the soil.

It's at this moment that my imagination fixes on Cadmus, alone on a strange continent, on a wild plain, the corpses of his men, the corpse of the dragon rotting on the long grass. He has a handful of dragon teeth, he has his nation-building mandate from the goddess. Did he hesitate? Did he savor the silence, the emptiness of the land? I think of him mustering the confidence for the dramatic gesture, with no one to witness it. He flings out his arm, the dragon teeth fly, their points turn downward midflight. They have the silhouette of dive bombers, the shadow of the colonizer, subduing the land by violence. The points embed themselves in the soil, armed men spring up, start fighting again, fresh blood spills on the bloodstained land. Cadmus and the survivors found the city of Thebes, and the blood continues to spill throughout its history: Pentheus, Oedipus—filicide, patricide, a history of taboo, passion, compulsion, and the rigid mandates of governing law.

I end the poem "Greenacre" when it seems like I've reached a stopping point, to keep the focus on the moment just prior to settlement, and the moment just after. But a seed has been planted in my mind, and it continues burrowing, growing. I find myself returning to the figure of Cadmus in later poems, the figure of the immigrant who is also the colonizer, who is successful by certain lights, who is cursed by certain lights. Sometimes when you write a poem, it opens doors to an infinite future of other poems.

Acknowledgments

Samuel Ace
"I met a man" appeared in *Our Weather Our Sea* (Black Radish Books, 2019).

Kaveh Akbar
"Reading Farrokhzad in a Pandemic" appeared in *Pilgrim Bell*. Copyright © 2021 by Kaveh Akbar. Reprinted with the permission of The Permissions Company LLC on behalf of Graywolf Press, graywolf press.org.

Rick Barot
"The Names" appeared in *The Galleons*. Copyright © 2020 by Rick Barot. Reprinted with the permission of The Permissions Company LLC on behalf of Milkweed Editions, milkweed.org.

Oliver Baez Bendorf
"Untitled [Who cut me from / growing into a buck?]" appeared in *The Spectral Wilderness* (Kent State University Press, 2015). Reprinted with the permission of the publisher.

Reginald Dwayne Betts
"House of Unending" appeared in *Felon: Poems*. Copyright © 2019 by Reginald Dwayne Betts. Reprinted with the permission of W.W. Norton & Company, Inc.

Mark Bibbins
"At the End of the Endless Decade" appeared on the Academy of American Poets Poem-a-Day. Reprinted with the permission of the author.

Jericho Brown
"Pause" appeared in *Please* (New Issues Poetry & Prose, 2008).

Rita Dove
"Götterdämmerung" appeared in *On the Bus with Rosa Parks*. Copyright © 1999 by Rita Dove. Reprinted with the permission of W.W. Norton & Company, Inc.

Camille T. Dungy
"Natural History" appeared in *Trophic Cascade* (Wesleyan University Press, 2017). Reprinted with the permission of the publisher.

Heid E. Erdrich
"The Theft Outright" appeared in *National Monuments* (Michigan State University Press, 2008). Reprinted with the permission of the author.

Martín Espada
"Haunt Me" appeared in *Vivas to Those Who Have Failed* (W.W. Norton, 2016). Reprinted with the permission of the author.

Tarfia Faizullah
"Great Material" appeared in *Registers of Illuminated Villages*. Copyright © 2018 by Tarfia Faizullah. Reprinted with the permission of The Permissions Company LLC on behalf of Graywolf Press, graywolfpress .org.

Jennifer Elise Foerster
"The Last Kingdom" appeared in *Bright Raft in the Afterweather*. Copyright © 2018 Jennifer Elise Foerster. Reprinted with the permission of the University of Arizona Press.

Carolyn Forché
"The Garden Shukkei-en" appeared in *The Angel of History*. Copyright © 1994 by Carolyn Forché. Reprinted with the permission of HarperCollins Publishers.

Rigoberto Gonzáles
"Anaberto FaceTimes with His Mother" appeared as "Anaberto Skypes with His Mother" in *Our Lady of the Crossword* (A Midsummer Night's Press, 2015). Reprinted with the permission of the publisher.

Jorie Graham
"Why" appeared in *To 2040* (Copper Canyon Press, 2023).

Ada Limón
"Adaptation" appeared in *Bright Dead Things*. Copyright © 2015 by Ada Limón. Reprinted with the permission of The Permissions Company LLC on behalf of Milkweed Editions, milkweed.org.

Cate Marvin
"My First Husband Was My Last" appeared in *Oracle: Poems*. Copyright © 2015 by Cate Marvin. Reprinted with the permission of W.W. Norton & Company, Inc.

Adrian Matejka
"On the B Side" appeared in *Somebody Else Sold the World*. Copyright © 2021 by Adrian Matejka. Reprinted with the permission of Penguin Books, an imprint of Penguin Publishing Group, a division of Penguin Random House LLC. All rights reserved.

Airea D. Matthews
"Sexton Texts Tituba from a Bird Conservatory" appeared in *Simulacra*. Copyright © 2017 by Airea D. Matthews. Reprinted with the permission of Yale University Press.

Eileen Myles
"My Boy's Red Hat" appeared in the anthology *Troubling the Line: Trans and Genderqueer Poetry and Poetics* (Nightboat Books, 2013).

Craig Santos Perez
"The Pacific Written Tradition" appeared in *Cream City Review* in 2016.

Robert Pinsky
"The Robots" appeared in *At the Foundling Hospital*. Copyright © 2016 by Robert Pinsky. Reprinted with the permission of Farrar, Straus and Giroux. All rights reserved.

D.A. Powell
"chronic" appeared in *Chronic*. Copyright © 2009 by D.A. Powell. Reprinted with the permission of The Permissions Company LLC on behalf of Graywolf Press, graywolfpress.org.

Roger Reeves
"Something About John Coltrane" appeared in *Best Barbarian*. Copyright © 2022 by Roger Reeves. Reprinted with the permission of W.W. Norton & Company, Inc.

Jason Reynolds
"April 17, 1942, Jackie Robinson Gets His First Major League Hit and We Still Us" appeared on iamjasonreynolds.com in 2018.

Erika L. Sánchez
"Saudade" appeared on the Academy of American Poets Poem-a-Day. Reprinted with the permission of the author.

Diane Seuss
"Still Life with Two Dead Peacocks and a Girl" appeared in *Still Life with Two Dead Peacocks and a Girl.* Copyright © 2018 by Diane Seuss. Reprinted with the permission of The Permissions Company LLC on behalf of Graywolf Press, graywolfpress.org.

Solmaz Sharif
"The Master's House" appeared in *Customs.* Copyright © 2018, 2022 by Solmaz Sharif. Reprinted with the permission of The Permissions Company LLC on behalf of Graywolf Press, graywolfpress.org.

Cedar Sigo
"A Handbook of Poetic Forms" appeared in *Royals.* Copyright © 2017 by Cedar Sigo. Reprinted with permission of the author and Wave Books.

Jake Skeets
"Maar" appeared in *Eyes Bottle Dark with a Mouthful of Flowers.* Copyright © 2019 by Jake Skeets. Reprinted with the permission of The Permissions Company LLC on behalf of Milkweed Editions, milkweed.org.

Danez Smith
"waiting on you to die so i can be myself" appeared in the *Los Angeles Review of Books.* Reprinted with the permission of the author.

Patricia Smith
"Sweet Daddy" appeared in *Big Towns, Big Talk* (Zoland Books, 1992). Reprinted with the permission of the author.

Arthur Sze
"Sleepers" appeared in *The Glass Constellation* (Copper Canyon Press, 2021).

About the Contributors

Samuel Ace is a trans and genderqueer poet and sound artist. He is the author most recently of *Our Weather Our Sea* and the newly reissued *Meet Me There: Normal Sex & Home in three days. Don't wash.* He is the recipient of the Astraea Lesbian Writer Award and the Firecracker Alternative Book Award in Poetry, as well as a multi-time finalist for the Lambda Literary Award and the National Poetry Series.

Kaveh Akbar is the author of *Pilgrim Bell* (Graywolf Press) and *Calling a Wolf a Wolf* (Alice James Books) and is editor of *The Penguin Book of Spiritual Verse.* Photo by Paige Lewis.

Rick Barot's most recent book of poems, *The Galleons,* was published by Milkweed Editions in 2020 and was longlisted for the National Book Award. His work has appeared in numerous publications, including *Poetry, The New Republic, Tin House, The Kenyon Review,* and *The New Yorker.* He has received fellowships from the Guggenheim Foundation, the National Endowment for the Arts, and Stanford University. He lives in Tacoma, Washington, and directs the Rainier Writing Workshop, the low-residency MFA program in creative writing at Pacific Lutheran University.

Oliver Baez Bendorf is the author of two books of poems, *Advantages of Being Evergreen* and *The Spectral Wilderness*. He has received fellowships and awards from the NEA and the Publishing Triangle. He founded and directs Spellworks and teaches in the low-residency MFA Program for Writers at Warren Wilson College. Born and raised in Iowa, he now lives in the Pacific Northwest.

Reginald Dwayne Betts is the founder and director of the Freedom Reads. A poet and lawyer, he is the author of four books and is a 2021 MacArthur Fellow. His latest collection of poetry, *Felon,* received the American Book Award and an NAACP Image Award. He holds a JD from Yale Law School.

Mark Bibbins is the author of four poetry collections, most recently *13th Balloon* (Copper Canyon Press, 2020), which received the Publishing Triangle's Thom Gunn Award. His first book, *Sky Lounge* (Graywolf Press, 2003), received a Lambda Literary Award. He lives in New York City and teaches in the graduate writing programs at the New School and Columbia University, and in NYU's Writers in Florence program.

Jericho Brown won the Pulitzer Prize for his most recent book, *The Tradition* (Copper Canyon, 2019). He is originally from Louisiana and now lives in Atlanta, Georgia.

Molly McCully Brown is the author of the essay collection *Places I've Taken My Body* (Persea Books, 2020), which was named a Kirkus Best Book of 2020, and the poetry collection *The Virginia State Colony for Epileptics and Feebleminded* (Persea, 2017), winner of the 2016 Lexi Rudnitsky First Book Prize. With Susannah Nevison, she is the coauthor of the poetry collection *In the Field Between Us* (Persea, 2020).

Her poems and essays have appeared in *The Paris Review, Tin House, The Yale Review, Virginia Quarterly Review, Crazyhorse, The New York Times,* and elsewhere. She is an assistant professor at Old Dominion University.

 Victoria Chang's latest book of poetry is *The Trees Witness Everything* (Copper Canyon Press). Her nonfiction book, *Dear Memory* (Milkweed Editions), was published in 2021. *Obit* (Copper Canyon, 2020) was named a New York Times Notable Book, a Time Must-Read Book, and received the Los Angeles Times Book Prize, the Anisfield-Wolf Book Award in Poetry, and the PEN/Voelcker Award. It was also longlisted for a National Book Award and named a finalist for the National Book Critics Circle Award and the Griffin International Poetry Prize. Chang has received a Guggenheim Fellowship, and she lives in Los Angeles. Photo by Rozette Rago.

 Jos Charles is author of the poetry collections *a Year & other poems* (Milkweed Editions, 2022), *feeld* (Milkweed, 2018), a Pulitzer finalist and winner of the 2017 National Poetry Series selected by Fady Joudah, and *Safe Space* (Ahsahta Press, 2016). She teaches in Randolph College's low-residency MFA program. Charles has an MFA from the University of Arizona and is currently a PhD student at UC Irvine. She resides in Long Beach, California. Photo by Sergio De La Torre.

 John Lee Clark is an award-winning DeafBlind poet and essayist whose latest book is *How to Communicate: Poems* (W.W. Norton, 2022). He is a Bush Leadership Fellow and travels extensively for work around the Protactile movement. He makes his home with his brilliant partner, the artist Adrean Clark; their three amazing roommates, aka their kids; and two feline collaborators.

Martha Collins has published eleven volumes of poetry, most recently *Casualty Reports* (University of Pittsburgh Press, 2022) and *Because What Else Could I Do* (Pittsburgh, 2019), which won the William Carlos Williams Award. She has also cotranslated five volumes of Vietnamese poetry, most recently *Dreaming the Mountain: Poems by Tuệ Sỹ* (Milkweed Editions, 2023). Collins founded the UMass Boston creative writing program and later taught at Oberlin College. She lives in Cambridge, Massachusetts.

 CAConrad has been working with the ancient technologies of poetry and ritual since 1975. Their new book is *Amanda Paradise: Resurrect Extinct Vibration* (Wave Books, 2021). They have received a Creative Capital Award, a Pew Fellowship, a Lambda Literary Award, and a Believer Magazine Book Award. Their play *The Obituary Show* was made into a film, in 2022, by Augusto Cascales. They teach at Columbia University in New York City and Sandberg Art Institute in Amsterdam. Photo by Augusto Cascales.

 Eduardo C. Corral is the son of Mexican immigrants. He's the author of *Guillotine* (Graywolf Press) and *Slow Lightning,* which won the 2011 Yale Series of Younger Poets competition. He's the recipient of a Guggenheim Fellowship, a Lannan Foundation Literary Fellowship, a Whiting Award, a National Endowment for the Arts Fellowship, and a Hodder Fellowship from Princeton University. He teaches in the MFA program at North Carolina State University.

 Laura Da' is a poet and teacher who studied at the Institute of American Indian Arts. She is the author of *Tributaries,* an American Book Award winner, and *Instruments of the True Measure,* a Washington State Book Award winner. Da' is Eastern Shawnee. She lives near Renton, Washington, with her family.

Oliver de la Paz is the author of six collections of poetry and editor of *A Face to Meet the Faces: An Anthology of Contemporary Persona Poetry.* He is a founding member of Kundiman and he teaches at the College of the Holy Cross and in the low-residency MFA Program at Pacific Lutheran University.

Mark Doty is the author of nine books of poetry, including *Deep Lane, Fire to Fire: New and Selected Poems,* which won the 2008 National Book Award, and *My Alexandria,* winner of the Los Angeles Times Book Prize, the National Book Critics Circle Award, and the T.S. Eliot Prize in the UK. He is also the author of four memoirs: the *New York Times*–bestselling *What Is the Grass, Dog Years, Firebird,* and *Heaven's Coast,* as well as a book about craft and criticism, *The Art of Description: World into Word,* and a critical meditation, *Still Life with Oysters and Lemon: On Objects and Intimacy.* Doty has received two NEA fellowships, Guggenheim and Rockefeller Foundation fellowships, a Lila Wallace–Readers Digest Award, and the Witter Bynner Prize. Photo by Paola Valenzuela.

Rita Dove received the 1987 Pulitzer Prize in Poetry and served as US Poet Laureate from 1993 to 1995. She is the only poet honored with both the National Humanities Medal and the National Medal of Arts. Recent recognitions include the Wallace Stevens Award and the American Academy of Arts and Letters Gold Medal in Poetry. She teaches creative writing at the University of Virginia; her latest poetry collection, *Playlist for the Apocalypse,* appeared in 2021.

Camille T. Dungy is the author of four collections of poetry, most recently *Trophic Cascade,* and the essay collection *Guidebook to Relative Strangers: Journeys into Race, Motherhood and History.* She has edited three anthologies, including *Black Nature: Four Centuries of African American*

Nature Poetry. Her honors include an Academy of American Poets Fellowship, a Guggenheim Fellowship, NEA Fellowships in both poetry and prose, and an American Book Award. Photo by Beowulf Sheehan.

Heid E. Erdrich's collection *Little Big Bully* is a winner of the National Poetry Series and the Balcones Prize. She edited *New Poets of Native Nations,* which won an American Book Award. Recent fellowships are from the Native Arts and Cultures Foundation and the Loft Literary Center. Heid is Ojibwe enrolled at Turtle Mountain.

Martín Espada has published more than twenty books as a poet, editor, essayist, and translator. His latest book of poems is called *Floaters,* winner of the 2021 National Book Award. Other books of poems include *Vivas to Those Who Have Failed* (2016), *The Trouble Ball* (2011), and *Alabanza* (2003). He has received the Ruth Lilly Poetry Prize, the Shelley Memorial Award, an Academy of American Poets Fellowship, and a Guggenheim Fellowship. Espada is a professor of English at UMass Amherst. www.martinespada.net

Tarfia Faizullah is the author of *Registers of Illuminated Villages* (Graywolf Press, 2018) and *Seam* (Southern Illinois University Press, 2014). Her writing appears widely in the US and abroad and has been translated into several languages. She is the recipient of a Fulbright Fellowship, three Pushcart Prizes, and other honors. Tarfia lives in Dallas, Texas.

Jennifer Elise Foerster is the author of three books of poetry, *Leaving Tulsa, Bright Raft in the Afterweather,* and *The Maybe-Bird.* She has been the recipient of a NEA Creative Writing Fellowship, a Lannan Foundation Residency Fellowship, and a Wallace Stegner Fellowship at Stanford University. A member of the Muscogee Nation, she lives in San Francisco.

Carolyn Forché is a poet, memoirist, translator, and editor. Her most recent works include *In the Lateness of the World*, a finalist for the Pulitzer Prize in Poetry and winner of an American Book Award, and her memoir *What You Have Heard Is True: A Memoir of Witness and Resistance*, which won the Juan E. Mendez Book Award for Human Rights in Latin America and was a finalist for the 2019 National Book Award in Nonfiction, the Dayton Literary Peace Prize, and the James Tait Black Prize in the United Kingdom. She is a professor in the Department of English at Georgetown University and has been a human rights activist for fifty years.

Rigoberto González is distinguished professor of English and director of the MFA Program in Creative Writing at Rutgers–Newark. A Lannan, Guggenheim, and USA Rolón Fellow, his latest publication is *To the Boy Who Was Night: New and Selected Poems*.

Jorie Graham is the author of fifteen collections, including most recently, *[To] The Last [Be] Human* and *To 2040*, both from Copper Canyon Press. Her work has been widely translated and is the recipient of numerous awards, including the Pulitzer Prize, the Los Angeles Times Book Prize, the Forward Prize (UK), the International Nonino Prize, and the Wallace Stevens Award. She teaches at Harvard and lives in Massachusetts. Photo by Jeannette Montgomery Barron.

Paul Guest is the author of four collections of poetry, most recently *Because Everything Is Terrible*, and a memoir, *One More Theory About Happiness*. His writing has appeared in *The American Poetry Review, Poetry, The Paris Review, Tin House, Slate, New England Review, The Southern Review, The Kenyon Review, Western Humanities Review, Ploughshares*, and numerous other publications. A Guggenheim Fellow and Whiting Award winner, he lives in Charlottesville, Virginia.

Kimiko Hahn casts a wide net for subject matter. In her collection *Foreign Bodies,* she revisits the personal as political while exploring the immigrant body, the endangered animal's body, objects removed from children's bodies, hoarded things, and charms. Previous books *Toxic Flora* and *Brain Fever* were prompted by fields of science; *The Narrow Road to the Interior* takes title and forms from Basho's famous journals. Honors include a Guggenheim Fellowship, PEN/ Voelcker Award, and the Shelley Memorial Award. Hahn is a distinguished professor in the MFA Program in Creative Writing & Literary Translation at Queens College, City University of New York.

francine j. harris's third collection, *Here Is the Sweet Hand* (FSG), was a finalist for the Kingsley Tufts Award and winner of the 2020 National Book Critics Circle Award. Her second collection, *play dead,* was the winner of the Lambda Literary and Audre Lorde Awards and finalist for the Hurston/Wright Legacy Award. Her first collection, *allegiance,* was a finalist for the Kate Tufts Discovery and PEN Open Book Awards. Originally from Detroit, she has received fellowships from the National Endowment for the Arts, the MacDowell Colony, and the Cullman Center for Scholars and Writers at the New York Public Library. She is an associate professor of English at the University of Houston and serves as consulting faculty editor at *Gulf Coast.*

Brenda Hillman's eleventh collection from Wesleyan University Press is *In a Few Minutes Before Later* (2022). A recent recipient of the Morton Dauwen Zabel Award from the American Academy of Arts and Letters, Hillman is a Chancellor Emerita of the Academy of American Poets and lives in the San Francisco Bay Area, where she teaches part-time at Saint Mary's College of California. Photo by Garret Hongo.

Tyehimba Jess is the author of two books of poetry, *Leadbelly* and *Olio. Olio* won the 2017 Pulitzer Prize, the Anisfield-Wolf Book Award, and the Midland Authors Award in Poetry; received an Outstanding Contribution to Publishing citation from the Black Caucus of the American Library Association; and was nominated for the National Book Critics Circle Award, the PEN/Jean Stein Book Award, and the Kingsley Tufts Poetry Award. Jess, a Cave Canem and NYU alumnus, received a 2004 Literature Fellowship from the National Endowment for the Arts, was a 2004–2005 Winter Fellow at the Fine Arts Work Center, and received the 2016 Lannan Award in Poetry. Photo by John Midgley.

Ilya Kaminsky is the author of *Deaf Republic* (Graywolf Press) and *Dancing in Odessa* (Tupelo Press). He is also the coeditor and cotranslator of several books, including *Ecco Anthology of International Poetry* (HarperCollins) and *Dark Elderberry Branch: Poems of Marina Tsvetaeva* (Alice James Books). Photo by Cybele Knowles, courtesy of the University of Arizona Poetry Center.

Donika Kelly is the author of *The Renunciations,* winner of the Anisfield-Wolf Book Award in Poetry, and *Bestiary,* the winner of the 2015 Cave Canem Poetry Prize, a Hurston/Wright Legacy Award for Poetry, and the Kate Tufts Discovery Award. A Cave Canem graduate fellow and a founding member of the collective Poets at the End of the World, she is an assistant professor at the University of Iowa.

Yusef Komunyakaa is the author of many books of poetry, including *Pleasure Dome, The Emperor of Water Clocks, The Chameleon Couch, Warhorses, Taboo, Talking Dirty to the Gods,* and *Neon Vernacular,* for which he received the Pulitzer Prize. His plays, performance art, and libretti have been performed internationally and include *Wakonda's*

Dream, Saturnalia, Testimony, and *Gilgamesh: A Verse Play.* His most recent collection is *Everyday Mojo Songs of Earth.* Photo by Arthur Elgort.

Pulitzer Prize finalist Dorianne Laux's most recent collection is *Only as the Day Is Long: New and Selected Poems* (W.W. Norton). She is also author of *The Book of Men,* winner of the Paterson Poetry Prize, and *Facts about the Moon,* winner of the Oregon Book Award. Laux teaches poetry at Pacific University. In 2020, she was elected a Chancellor of the Academy of American Poets.

Dana Levin's fifth book is *Now Do You Know Where You Are,* a New York Times Editors' Choice. A Guggenheim Fellow, Levin serves as Distinguished Writer in Residence at Maryville University in Saint Louis.

Ada Limón is the author of six books of poetry, including *The Carrying,* which won the National Book Critics Circle Award. Limón is also the host of the critically acclaimed poetry podcast *The Slowdown.* Her new book of poetry, *The Hurting Kind,* is out now from Milkweed Editions.

Cate Marvin is the author of four books of poems. *World's Tallest Disaster* (2001) and *Fragment of the Head of a Queen* (2007) were both published by Sarabande Books. Her third collection, *Oracle,* appeared from W.W. Norton in 2015. A recipient of a Whiting Award and a Guggenheim Fellowship, Marvin is a professor of English at the College of Staten Island, City University of New York. Her fourth book, *Event Horizon,* was published by Copper Canyon Press in 2022. She lives in southern Maine.

Adrian Matejka is the author of seven books, including a mixed-media collection inspired by Funkadelic, *Standing on the Verge & Maggot Brain* (Third Man Books, 2021); a collection of poems, *Somebody Else Sold the World* (Penguin Press, 2021), which was a finalist for 2022 UNT Rilke Prize; and the graphic novel *Last On His Feet* (Liveright, 2023). He lives in Chicago and is the editor of *Poetry* magazine.

Airea D. Matthews is the author of *Simulacra,* winner of the 2016 Yale Series of Younger Poets, and the collection *Bread and Circus* (2023). She is an associate professor at Bryn Mawr College, a yoga and meditation teacher, and a contemplative. She lives in Philadelphia, where she is the current poet laureate.

Eileen Myles (they/them) came to New York from Boston in 1974 to be a poet. Their books include *For Now, I Must Be Living Twice/new and selected poems* and *Chelsea Girls. Pathetic Literature* (2022), which they edited, is out from Grove. Eileen has received a Guggenheim Fellowship and in 2021 was elected a member of the American Academy of Arts and Letters. They live in New York and Marfa, Texas. Photo by Shae Detar.

Craig Santos Perez is an indigenous Chamoru from the Pacific Island of Guam. He has authored five books of poetry and is a professor at the University of Hawaiʻi at Mānoa.

Robert Pinsky's recent autobiography is *Jersey Breaks: Becoming an American Poet* (2022). His books of poetry include *At the Foundling Hospital, The Want Bone,* and *The Figured Wheel,* a finalist for the Pulitzer Prize. His best-selling translation is *The Inferno of Dante.* His Tanner

Lectures at Princeton were published as *Democracy, Culture and the Voice of Poetry.*

 D.A. Powell's books include *Repast: Tea, Lunch & Cocktails* (Graywolf Press, 2014) and *Useless Landscape, or A Guide for Boys* (Graywolf, 2012). His most recent collection is *Atlas T* (Rescue Press, 2020). A former Briggs-Copeland Lecturer at Harvard, Powell has taught at Columbia University, UT Austin, Stanford, and the University of Iowa. His work spans the personal, political, and pastoral and has received numerous awards and honors, including the 2019 John Updike Award from the American Academy of Arts and Letters, a National Book Critics Circle Award in Poetry, the California Book Award, and the Shelley Memorial Award from the Poetry Society of America. He lives in San Francisco and teaches at the University of San Francisco.

 Roger Reeves is the author of *King Me* and *Best Barbarian.* He is also the recipient of a National Endowment for the Arts Fellowship, a Ruth Lilly and Dorothy Sargent Rosenberg Fellowship from the Poetry Foundation, and a 2015 Whiting Award, among other honors. His work has appeared in *Poetry, The New Yorker, The Paris Review,* and elsewhere. He lives in Austin, Texas.

 Jason Reynolds is the author of more than a dozen books for young people, including *Look Both Ways: A Tale Told in Ten Blocks,* a National Book Award finalist that was named a Best Book of 2019 by NPR, *The New York Times, The Washington Post,* and *Time.* A native of Washington, DC, Reynolds began writing poetry at age nine and is the recipient of a Newbery Honor, a Printz Honor, an NAACP Image Award, and multiple Coretta Scott King Award honors. His book (with Ibram X. Kendi) *Stamped: Racism, Antiracism, and You,* was a #1 New York Times Bestseller. His most recent book is *Ain't Burned All the Bright,* with artwork by Jason Griffin. Reynolds was the 2020–2022 National Ambassador for Young People's Literature and has appeared on *The Daily Show with Trevor Noah, Late Night with Seth Meyers,* and *CBS Sunday Morning.* He is on faculty at Lesley University, for the Writing for Young People MFA Program. You can find his ramblings at JasonWritesBooks.com. Photo by Adedayo "Dayo" Kosoko.

Erika L. Sánchez is the author of *Lessons on Expulsion, I Am Not Your Perfect Mexican Daughter,* and *Crying in the Bathroom.*

Diane Seuss is the author of five books of poetry. Her most recent collection is *frank: sonnets* (Graywolf Press, 2021), winner of the PEN/Voelcker Prize, the Los Angeles Times Book Prize, the National Book Critics Circle Award for Poetry, and the Pulitzer Prize. *Still Life with Two Dead Peacocks and a Girl* (Graywolf, 2018) was a finalist for the National Book Critics Circle Award and the Los Angeles Times Book Prize in Poetry. *Four-Legged Girl* (Graywolf, 2015) was a finalist for the Pulitzer Prize. Her sixth collection, *Modern Poetry,* is forthcoming from Graywolf Press in 2024. Seuss is a 2020 Guggenheim Fellow. She received the John Updike Award from the American Academy of Arts and Letters in 2021. Seuss was raised by a single mother in rural Michigan, which she continues to call home. Photo by Gabrielle Montesanti.

Solmaz Sharif is the author of *Customs* and *Look.* Her work has appeared in *The New Yorker, Harper's, The New York Times, The Paris Review,* and elsewhere. She is currently an assistant professor at Arizona State University, where she directs a Poetry for the People program.

Cedar Sigo is a poet and member of the Suquamish Tribe. He studied writing and poetics at Naropa University. His most recent books are *All This Time* (poetry) and *Guard the Mysteries* (lectures), both published by Wave Books in 2021. In 2022, he received a Grants to Artists Award from the Foundation for Contemporary Arts. He is the editor of *There You Are: Interviews, Journals & Ephemera* by Joanne Kyger. He was an advisory editor with Joy Harjo on *When the Light of the World Was Subdued Our Songs Came Through: A Norton Anthology of Native Nations Poetry.*

 Jake Skeets is the author of *Eyes Bottle Dark with a Mouthful of Flowers,* winner of the National Poetry Series, the Kate Tufts Discovery Award, the American Book Award, and the Whiting Award. He is from the Navajo Nation and teaches at Diné College. He joined the University of Oklahoma as an assistant professor in 2022.

 Danez Smith is the author of three collections, including *Homie* and *Don't Call Us Dead.* Their work has been awarded the UK's Forward Prize for Best Collection, the Minnesota Book Award in Poetry, and the Kate Tufts Discovery Award, and has been a finalist for the NAACP Image Award in Poetry, the National Book Critics Circle Award, and the National Book Award. Former host of the *VS* podcast, they live in Minneapolis near their people.

 Patricia Smith is the author of *Incendiary Art,* winner of the Ruth Lilly Prize for Lifetime Achievement from the Poetry Foundation, the Kingsley Tufts Award, the Los Angeles Times Book Prize, and the NAACP Image Award and finalist for the Pulitzer Prize; *Shoulda Been Jimi Savannah,* winner of the Lenore Marshall Prize from the Academy of American Poets; and *Blood Dazzler,* a National Book Award finalist.

She is a visiting professor at Princeton University and a distinguished professor for the City University of New York.

Arthur Sze has published eleven books of poetry, including *The Glass Constellation: New and Collected Poems* (Copper Canyon Press, 2021) and *Sight Lines,* which won the 2019 National Book Award for Poetry. Sze also received the 2021 Shelley Memorial Award from the Poetry Society of America, and he is a professor emeritus at the Institute of American Indian Arts. He lives in Santa Fe, New Mexico.

Mary Szybist is the author of *Granted* (Alice James Books), a finalist for the National Book Critics Circle Award, and *Incarnadine* (Graywolf Press), winner of the 2013 National Book Award for Poetry. She lives in Portland, Oregon, where she teaches at Lewis & Clark College.

Ocean Vuong is the author of the novel *On Earth We're Briefly Gorgeous* (Penguin Press, 2019), and the poetry collections *Night Sky with Exit Wounds* (Copper Canyon Press, 2016) and *Time Is a Mother* (Penguin, 2022). A recipient of a 2019 MacArthur Fellowship, he currently lives in Northampton, Massachusetts, and serves as a tenured professor in the NYU Creative Writing Program. Photo by Tom Hines.

Monica Youn is the author of *From From, Blackacre, Ignatz,* and *Barter.* She has been a finalist for the National Book Award, the National Book Critics Circle Award, and the Kingsley Tufts Award and has been awarded the William Carlos Williams Prize, a Levinson Prize, a Guggenheim Fellowship, a Witter Bytter Fellowship, and a Stegner Fellowship. A former lawyer and a member of the Racial Imaginary Institute, she is a professor at UC Irvine.

About the Editors

Erin Belieu is the author of numerous poetry collections, all from Copper Canyon Press, including *Black Box,* a finalist for the Los Angeles Times Book Prize, *Slant Six,* chosen as one of the New York Times Book Critics' favorite books of 2014, and 2021's *Come-Hither Honeycomb.* Belieu's poems have appeared in places such as *The New Yorker, Poetry, The New York Times, The Atlantic,* the Academy of American Poets Poem-a-Day, *The American Poetry Review,* and *The Kenyon Review,* and have been selected for multiple appearances in the *Best American Poetry* series. A Rona Jaffe Fellow, winner of the Barnes and Noble Writers for Writers Award, and AWP's George Garrett Prize, Belieu is the founder of the literary resistance network Writers Resist. Belieu teaches for the University of Houston Creative Writing Program.

Carl Phillips is the author of sixteen books of poetry, most recently *Then the War: And Selected Poems, 2007–2020* (FSG, 2022), which won the Pulitzer Prize. Other honors include the 2021 Jackson Prize, the Aiken Taylor Award for Modern American Poetry, the Kingsley Tufts Award, a Lambda Literary Award, the PEN/USA Award for Poetry, and fellowships from the Guggenheim Foundation, the Library of Congress, the American Academy of Arts and Letters, and the Academy of American Poets. Phillips has also written three prose books, most recently *My Trade Is Mystery: Seven Meditations from a Life in Writing* (Yale University Press, 2022), and he has translated the *Philoctetes* of Sophocles (Oxford University Press, 2004). He teaches at Washington University in St. Louis.

Poetry is vital to language and living. Since 1972, Copper Canyon Press has published extraordinary poetry from around the world to engage the imaginations and intellects of readers, writers, booksellers, librarians, teachers, students, and donors.

WE ARE GRATEFUL FOR THE MAJOR SUPPORT PROVIDED BY:

academy of
american poets

THE PAUL G. ALLEN
FAMILY FOUNDATION

Lannan

TO LEARN MORE ABOUT UNDERWRITING
COPPER CANYON PRESS TITLES,
PLEASE CALL 360-385-4925 EXT. 103

WE ARE GRATEFUL FOR THE MAJOR SUPPORT PROVIDED BY:

Richard Andrews and
    Colleen Chartier
Anonymous
Jill Baker and Jeffrey Bishop
Anne and Geoffrey Barker
Donna Bellew
Will Blythe
John Branch
Diana Broze
John R. Cahill
Sarah Cavanaugh
Keith Cowan and Linda Walsh
Stephanie Ellis-Smith and
    Douglas Smith
Mimi Gardner Gates
Gull Industries Inc.
    on behalf of William True
William R. Hearst III
Carolyn and Robert Hedin
David and Jane Hibbard
Bruce S. Kahn
Phil Kovacevich and Eric Wechsler

Lakeside Industries Inc.
    on behalf of Jeanne Marie Lee
Maureen Lee and Mark Busto
Ellie Mathews and Carl Youngmann
    as The North Press
Larry Mawby and Lois Bahle
Hank and Liesel Meijer
Petunia Charitable Fund and
    adviser Elizabeth Hebert
Madelyn S. Pitts
Suzanne Rapp and Mark Hamilton
Adam and Lynn Rauch
Emily and Dan Raymond
Joseph C. Roberts
Cynthia Sears
Kim and Jeff Seely
D.D. Wigley
Barbara and Charles Wright
In honor of C.D. Wright,
    from Forrest Gander
Caleb Young as C. Young Creative
The dedicated interns and faithful
    volunteers of Copper Canyon Press

The pressmark for Copper Canyon Press suggests
entrance, connection, and interaction
while holding at its center
an attentive, dynamic space for poetry.

This book is set in Reminga Pro.
Book design by Gopa & Ted2, Inc.
Printed on archival-quality paper.